A Small Journal
of Heroin Addiction

Autobiographical writings by
Robin Marchesi

Clocktower Books
C&C Publishers
San Diego, CA

CLOCKTOWER
Books
San Diego, CA

www.clocktowerbooks.com

Copyright ©2000 by Robin Marchesi. All Rights Reserved.

Cover art and design by Brian Callahan.

CLOCKTOWER and design are trademarks of C&C Publishers.

ISBN 0-7433-0052-1

Author's Introduction

This book is my personal journal, parts of it crabbed into a makeshift notebook with a pencil stub while I sat in a sun-bleached Spanish prison two decades ago, parts of it typed on a modern computer in the comfort of central London. This book—these two books, these journals, I should say—are subjective, they are poetic, they are intimate. They tell of a horrifying dance between nightmare and redemption.

The first, composed 1979 and entitled Los Rosales, charts a six week period when I had the opportunity to explore my life and addictions, under unique circumstances. It began in Amsterdam, a haven of druggies and hippies in the 70's, and it follows my journey to Ceuta, where I got some space in hell, to take a good look at where I was and what I'd become. I made no allowance for an audience. I wrote to save my sanity, to try and make some sense of the depths to which I'd plunged. When I returned to London my manuscript like myself was not taken very seriously. I buried my journal in an old suitcase but never lost faith in its content. I like to think it has matured like a good wine, or grown strong roots in the dark of the earth. It lives and breathes in the year 2000 touching themes at the heart of the world today, as much as the world in which it was created.

In 1999 I wrote Mission. The circumstances were very different from those portrayed in Los Rosales. I was not lurching and stumbling through my days. I went to Northern California, older and no longer a junkie. I was concerned with another person's heroin addiction, on another continent. I was the victim rather than the perpetrator and there was a poetic justice in my position. On reflection, Mission paid a karmic debt I incurred while writing Los Rosales and only when I returned to England and began working on the journal, did I see the connection and continuity they gave each other.

The stories speak with their own voice, loud and clear. The pivotal theme of heroin addiction is a starting point for a much larger canvas that explores many timeless social and philosophic themes, as well as themes that relate to all personal families, friends and lovers. The journals are multi layered and I've retained much of their original form, moving between prose and poetry to illustrate the way a mind, swiftly and silently dances along to its internal movie.

I was given no commission for these undertakings nor were there any preconceptions in their composition. They fit together through an accident of time and space rather than any intentional force. It is they, not I, who direct this narrative.

We think that we manipulate events, but are we not manipulated by events?
We think we go to meet that which we experience, but that which we experience may come to meet us.
It is perhaps an illusion that we 'live':
We are 'lived'."

Wei Wu Wei: Finger Pointing at the Moon, 1958.

Part One

LOS ROSALES

Amsterdam...Easter 1979.

The further out the point the easier to write.
Tired, hungry, full of apprehensions, nervous tensions.

This city has always been good to me. It treats me as a guest and puts me in warm American Hotels. I feel privileged here always have done.
A writer writing words,
Presented with the necessary environment to write.
Thank you.
Very obliged for the opportunity.

I feel filled with madness; yet within runs some strangely hypnotic logic that enhances an already believable magic,
Making life
Appear tragic.

I am what I am.
I do what I do.
Boo Hoo to you too..
For being in misery woe.
'Cos minds not comfortable
Not knowing
Directions.

Awful backache
Living a nostalgia
No time to contemplate,
'Cept now,
In this city—Good to me.

Every time I arrive, this city gives all its got and I end up a rich man.

Rich with madness and misfortune.

Re/veiled with starlight, aching for the answers within life, presented with the tools of my trade in a city cushioned with flowers, canals, heroin, hotels that play T.V./Radio and serve late meals.

I write in between the balcony and dawn, aching, poor yet rich in mystery.

Surrounded by domes, diamonds, drugs, dreams and noise.

City so good to me.

A turning point place.

Sky bleeds grey boats, wisps of gaseous air.

Evening shed a storm.

I sneeze in recollection.

Rain bowed splash of night light.

Aching back, from the heroin come down. How after eighteen months rehabilitation did I allowed myself to slip back into 'smack' again? Now I'm in no mans land. Not knowing which way to go. Caught between a pretence of being cured, or picking up the pieces of what went before. Or maybe just leaving it all behind, Oxford, London, England. Let the writing write me.

At the back of the Station here in Amsterdam, past several tram lines and two canals, they have a street like Gerrard Street in London. In seedy neon lit windows, curvaceous girls display their sexual innuendoes while their pimps sell smack, to those not interested in female knickers. Last time I was here I got ripped off in an alley way, nearby this street (or rather a strasse). I returned to a similar room to this one, and looked dolefully at the package of cat litter. On this street they rip you off. I resist temptation. Sun fades and bows to cloud shadow. The sound of trams.

I reflect on my flat mate in Oxford. Francis, the young earnest art student who believes so sincerely in the 'Rehab' philosophy.

How he hated it when I compared him to Van Gogh.
Perhaps he thought his Art wasn't worth an ear.
Tick Tock
Ticking clock.
Turning point place
Space to find a direction.

Will I hang on or will I crack up further and risk a rip off on the street?
Score...
Maybe I should go to New York.
I could go to Ibiza, London, Oxford, Rome,
Or stay here
In the rich city. Good to me.
A turning point place
Laced with diamonds.

Trains - Boats - Planes -
Travel - Travel - Travel
Seeking a homeward road
With no home to go too.
'Cept where one finds oneself,
In a moment.
Be it the turning point place,
Paris, Rome, Rio,
26,000 feet in the air
On some steam boat
Marching the Oceans advance,
Or on a train
Voyaging through the heart of England

On a sun shining resurrection day
With children's laughter,
Rustling an overtone to the beat of wheels
On Iron.

I return to Henry Road, a small side street in North Oxford near the leafy suburb of Botley. I share this house with two men whom I met in Rehabilitation and a young waitress. Since my relapse the atmosphere toward me has become frosty. There is an air of solemnity in the small sitting room.
I want to make a phone call but there is a note on the phone.
It says: "PLEASE record all calls !!"
It is aimed at me,
The un recorder.
I become too paranoid to pick up the receiver.
Instead I stare at cold sunlight
On blank walls
And in this verse
Attempt to emulate
Leonard Cohen's depression,
So I may feel justified
In dialling a number.................

I ran out of Heroin
Thought about its warmth.
I ran out of hashish
Thought about its dream.
I ran out of nicotine
And realised what it means
To no longer be
A drug addict.

I lay down my pen and pick up the telephone............

"I ran into Judy yesterday, " says the receiver, reminding me of my old lover. "She's gone to Spain. Why don't you pay her a visit.....? Just a suggestion. Better than visiting me for you know what. How long will you be ?"
"Three hours."
"See you then."
The phone goes dead.

I replenish my suitcase and leave Oxford.

MAY 1979. VICTORIA STATION.

Stench of puke on unwashed bodies. Breath clogged, faces craggy. The urinal has been crapped in. Faeces float alongside Mc Kewens Export cans and piss. In the cafe the floor is spattered with caked, ingrained dirt. An old asthmatic drops used paper cups into a dustbin liner. Grudgingly sniffs as he puts plates on a nicotine-stained trolley. Train queue five hundred yards long. Words sprayed from lips laced with spittle. Talk of sex, sin, Thatcher, money, all in fantasy.

I say good bye to you,
London town,
And you like an abused lover
Reveal the ugliness
Beneath your facade.

TRAIN BARCELONA—MALAGA MAY 1979.

Every moment must be savoured
Every point taken

Sharpen the wits,
For mountains to North
Seas to the South.
What sights to see
Perceive them for what they be !

Sunset on western sky. Rolling Stones play on small cassette. Black mountains silhouette horizon. Dusty southern sparseness. Train rocks rhythmically. A Moroccan shows me how to set alight, ones own hand with out pain.

"Please to meet you. Hope you guess my name," added the tape recorder. Flowers reflect on by passing train's window, flashing shadows, a burst of evening sun. One perfectly angled beam shoots into me. A fix for life. I have travelled 1,000 miles ostensibly to intense detriment, following some primeval call. Let it be. The Magic Gather.

FOR JUDY. MALAGA MAY '79.

Travelled 1000 miles to see you and when I knocked on your door you were gone. What happened I wonder ? Perhaps you feared, like I, a meeting. The chemistry of our beings was beyond this moment in time, at any rate, explosive. Together we witnessed the death of your parents and my closest friend. Yet......

Indeed, for eternity I may cast back my mind to meet you. As if joined by some inexplicable bond which began before our bodies began, we in the degradation of those chaotic times formed a bond unbreakable in spirit, so that at any given moment I may present to any stranger a piece of you and you may present a piece of me. Some little personality trait picked up unconsciously as we both strove towards some ultimate beauty formed out of an intense degradation.

So 1000 miles I came to find you out but in my mind.

I guess it doesn't matter. Maybe 'tis meant to be this way. That finally I should decide to pack it all in and go on my own journey. I search like billions of others for peace, contentment, happiness. Some form of respite from the dour, inescapable industrialism of Europe. The factory bilge and worthless plastics peddled and pushed on peoples. A payment; so that in judgement people may say—"I knew no better, merely did what I was told was right."

"Democracy = Freedom by fear ." Free to do as you want within the confines of democratic institutions. Fear of going outside these institutions, for outside is the unknown elsewhere an area which may be worse than democratic institutions. We are taught this is so. Fear of failure, poverty, self discovery, being on one's own. Indeed being on one's own is the only way to be. Fear of non-material life—Better in most peoples cases to be 'liberal' or 'democratic'; rather than look into yourself, in order to explore and comprehend one's own species.

Ship glides over blue waters;

Gulls ghosts in slipstream.

Flash of sun on silver pen

Caught a train from Barcelona to Malaga. Twenty four hours with two Austrians and a Moroccan. Very strange journey through Spanish hinterland. Sparse feudal countryside. Stunted trees bearing lemons, olives, oranges. Dust, dirt, the worst toilets ever encountered. Even the passageways on this train were blocked with peasant poverty. I wonder if the battles fought in the Catalonian forests had gone to the Communists, would these people be more contented with some forty years of rigorous socialism ? Would the peoples plough and horse be replaced by combined harvester and tractor ? Would the valleys be aglow with electric towns ?

The mountains, valleys and streams; poppies like flashes of colour in the clean air. The train clambered the hillsides and descended precariously to the city. The Austrians talked of Morocco of the peace, stillness and hashish.

I came 1000 miles to talk with you
'Bout battles inside my head.
Hoping maybe to once more
Lay my weary self on your breasts
And explain my dream.
I came 1000 miles to find you
And you were out,
But
In my mind.

Morocco. A destination. Influenced by the two Austrians on the train I followed their advice up to a small village known locally as 'Ba-d- Idee'. Score half a kilo of fair hashish with my last money and then take a bus here the last resting place before the enclave of Ceuta and its customs post.

Flies, dirt, another thick black coffee before I slip over the border. I dream of Santa Eulalia del Rio, Ibiza where I intend to profit from my business, otherwise this whole literary event may disappear in a puff of proverbial smoke and I shall be repatriated for being a deranged tramp. Heart in mouth I join the throng who walk over a rickety bridge. In the distance lies the Mediterranean. Only one small obstacle between me and a Balearic Island. I pull down my peaked cap and make my way to the awaiting officials.

CEUTA PRISON JUNE '79.

What a turn up for the books. Busted at Ceuta ! Sat here, surrounded by roses waiting for administrative details to be completed, and then sentence...Half a kilo. Too much of nothing. Manage to steal half an ounce back though the guards seem trigger happy, twirling their guns at the slightest twitch. What a bummer ! They kept me overnight in a cell with straw, where a half mad alcoholic seems to have shit. Still I guess 'tis all for the best, as far as the 'master plan' 'tis concerned...Wham....Bam...Misery woe....A hopeless case for this sun tanned face.

In the morning I'm taken to an old fort at the highest point of the town. The Gaol, visible from miles around from the outside but an enclosure, designed to keep its tenants well incarcerated. "Los Rosales", the Roses is the ironic title for this Foreign Legionnaire.
Shadow moves from East to West.
An inanimate
Of the Institution.

Put in large dormitory type room with all the other Europeans. A five star hotel compared to the night on itchy straw. There are similar dormitories for Spaniards, for Moroccans and for deserters from the Legion. These dormitories are called *brigadas*.

Red light; glow of orange reflection on dappled floor.
Silence blends with harmonica's harmony.
Dusty Spanish evening.
Bread, water, hashish internationale.
Maybe the springboard to another direction ?...

"May auld acquaintance be forgot..." hums the harmonica. The player of this mouth organed tune is called Army. He sits crossed legged, yoga style on his bed, head shaved like a Buddha. I learn quickly he is a young German who ran away from his homeland, after killing someone. In his desperation he joined the Spanish Foreign Legion. He deserted, got caught and now plays harmonica as he awaits deportation. He seems frail with a very far away look, in his Aryan blue eyes.
Every one has a story to tell;
Every dream 'tis dreamed.
The summer dust, a simple lust.
Desire
A force precise
An incision

Into the depths of being.

Morning, sun, courtyard, shadows, skin flakes dry. Melodic *Tranquillo*. A gesture in the white aridness of a desert.
Ceuta, the end of the world, silver moonbeams, space to be.
I've come over 1500 miles
And here
In the depths of the human quagmire
I begin to perceive
Salvation.

These stories
This collection
To you the reader, now
'Tis only one man's perception in recollection.
Moments spent within his own walls.
Maybe true,
Maybe
Merely stories
Fantasies
Make believe
Fairy tales for Mankind.

Evening
Sunset
Candle light
Sound of a creaking bed
The softness of a brush through hair
Genesis play on the Radio.
A Moroccan in the next door *brigada* screams.
Spanish legionnaires,

Snoring out their transit and fate
For desertion.
The dust of deserts
The shadow of winged angels
A skeleton cross spoon,
Visions in the moonlight.
Candle lit,
Baying dogs,
Stars at Los Rosales
The Roses.

If you don't understand
And believe your mis comprehension
Is mine, (the writers) fault,
For failing to express
A correct interpretation,
I apologize,
For these words
Are incomprehensible
As merely words.
They are paintings, captured prisms of man's moment. Reflections of a whole,
For your, (the reader's) interpretation.

BON CHANCE !

Cold light of day
Grey clouds
Biting wind
On back of neck
Sound of water running from tap.
Voices talking conversations,
Conversed a night ago
In the granite, cobbled courtyard
Of another sun filled day.

Surprising how dull the weather is here in the morning. The overcast sky wearing an overcoat for the sun.

We spend about two thirds of the day on a rough and uneven courtyard, whose undulations help create huge puddles, or miniature ponds. About a third of this square *'patio'*, (as it's known), is underwater. The water coagulates and derives from a large sink with a hole in the bottom. Here 200 people wash clothes, drink, piss, whatever they need to do. The wastage gathers in the uneven surface. The yard is covered with old paper and cigarette ends, even cracks in the sandy walls contain pieces of rubbish. In a corner lies a huge refuse stack from which, occasionally flicking out of its container, more garbage is distributed in the cool wind. Like us prisoners. One day, they just come along and let us free. Flick us out of the rubbish heap into the mainstream, to mainline humanity with a fix, from Ceuta!

A brief summary of the linear time events at Los Rosales.

Day begins early at 7.30, with a shrill whistle blown by one of the officers, known here as *'Functionales'*. Our *brigada* is unlocked by a deformed Moroccan blue band. We descend quickly and assemble, in the early morning shadow of the Courtyard for a head count. After this we partake of breakfast. One roll and a cup of tea. There is a small shop where one can buy coffee and food. Most people sit on the long granite benches which are the first places for the sun to hit, when it clambers over the prison wall. Four and a half hours later about twelve, if the sun remains constant and if the clouds clear, the Courtyard is a brilliantly blared reflection of the blue sky.

Lunch is at one. More white bread. Bowl of soup. Some indefinable meat. An orange. At two thirty, we return to the *brigada* for Siesta. At 5:30 p.m. we once more return to the Courtyard and another head count. We sit at that time, on the granite benches, directly opposite the ones we occupied in the morning. We watch the sun disappear behind the Western Wall of the Fort. At eight o' clock, we return upstairs for the night after another inedible meal. The evening can be long and sleep comes about one in the morning.

There's the day at Los Rosales. But really its what goes on in between which is important. The talks, the games, the thoughts, perceptions, hopes and fears within. The world of inner space, where each individual weaves their own webs. The tangible-time-table objective realism, that people seem so certain is the way to contentment, is quite superficial, to what goes on in a moment shared between individuals.
Be it a minute or a lifetime.
A Rose or Los Rosales......

One man stands,
Between the cook house and basins.
He plays with a baton,
Twirling skilfully the instrument.
Writing signs on the invisible
With each shift of his adroit fingers.
I ask about him.
A Deserter From the Spanish Legion.
All he knows, is the Desert air.
He hears
Only the sound of distant bugles.
One hand, rigidly by his side.

Feet at attention.
Leading the Brigade
To victory.

I would like, very much, to get away from here. I would like to bathe in the clean Mediterranean. Then I would shower and put on clean clothes. I'd go out for a pleasant meal, served in tasteful surroundings. After coffee, I would excuse myself and go to the toilet. This place would be quiet and full of flowers. In these lush surroundings, I would take a long clean fix of morphine.

I don't know really what I'm doing. Look at me. A 28 year old junkie. The longest stretch of work I've done for the system in my country is six months. Since the age of 18 I've either been a student (three times), on bail (twice), already once in prison and through a resocialisation process in the Rehabilitation centre. A total failure to friends and family alike. Yes! I have run away and ended up here at Ceuta with all the other so called failures and no goods. All I've ever done consistently is write little rhymes. Sometimes it's poetry, sometimes prose, sometimes riddles or magic spells. However they are something. A little individualistic contribution indeed a unique injection of language.

'Tis words, their fascination, their magic and movement that have ensnared me.

They have guided and controlled my destiny. All I have is my use of language and fate demands me, to experience what I experience, for its own flow within the whole. I, deceiving no one, follow, whilst those around me weep tears, for my redemption !

Dire Straits play on the Radio. The Italian, Bruno, deals the cards. I wonder about my Mother and Father. Depression. Listening to the world of the dead. Think I've spent more time in the land of voiceless being, than in the land of the living, lately. Hearing the call. My parents, no doubt will be really disappointed at my present position. 'Tis so sad. The lino on the *brigada* floor. Foreign faces. Dreams. Some vague vision..

"How long?... How much longer Lord ?"

"For eternity, my son. Till people learn of humanity...."

Birds call, canaries,

Bruno, the Italian,

Deals the last card.

Tired, hungry, lonely, cold. Army, the Harmonica playing murderer whom nobody crosses plays an old tune from my childhood:

"Show me the way to go home,

'Cos I'm tired and I wanna go to bed......"

Goes the lyric. I remember these lines from when I was six, walking at dusk to the light warmth of my family womb. In the twilight a drunken man lurching.

"I had a little drink just an hour ago,

And its gone right to my head...."

I remember my vision. A lantern, tall grass, and a sad man looking for something he needs but doesn't have.

"Where ever I may roam, " continues the lyric,

"On land or sea or foam

"I'll just keep on singing this song,

"Show me the way to go home......"

With no home to go too.

I had a funny little dream last night interspersed by itching. Something to do with the blankets. The sun attempting to break through clouds. Awake. Sound of jangling keys. This morning really cold during head count. A biting wind which borders on a stiff breeze, consistently blowing clouds across the blue horizon. No sun tan for this pale face.

I am beginning to distinguish the groups of people in the *brigada*. There is a national sub division which is quite diverse. Five Germans, six French, ten Italians, a Russian and four English. This balance may fluctuate upon the efficiency of Spanish customs, but our common crime gives us a unity. We are an E.E.C. of hashish.

As a new boy I don't get on so well with the other English. They seem to live in a fantasy always talking of smuggling, 'scamming' for the future. No doubt it's a diversion to our daily plod around the courtyard, but they seem to think they know it all. At least, I know that if any of us knew anything, we wouldn't be here. Yes. Last night I crossed swords with the arrogant, Paul. When I made some remark about the funding of his openly discussed enterprise, he suggested I use my manuscript as shit paper. He contributes nothing but self importance and a 'You owe me' attitude, without offering anything. I threatened to hit him if he carried on being so impolite. He stopped. I know his kind of middle class hippie, awaiting optimistically, someone finding 10 million pesetas or you rot for five years and you can't deal with this reality, so each day you add to your fantasy in the hope of filling time as it passes you by.

Taffy, the Welshman, in this area of fantasy/reality is worse than Paul. He has done two out of six years and is hoping for an amnesty. He is about forty and by my reckoning, his scam will cost more than it can make. When I suggested this fundamental flaw in his very expensive, impracticable scheme, he said first I'm not a smuggler and second money to him was, "No Problem." He says he won't listen to me 'cos I'm a junkie. Maybe after Taffy has finished his six years, he'll make it. I don't know, but there must be a lot of Taffy types, in prisons all over the world.

The Russian, Joseph, is a classic "cool." Maybe in his mid fifties and a total loner. There seems something odd about a communist hashish seller, but he tells me some of the best hashish comes from the steppes of the Balkan Mountains. It seems, during the evening as he sits on his bed looking at the various groups through his piercing eyes and puffing on a large cigar, that he sees straight through everyone. He it is, who runs this European quarter. He is the dealer, the psychologist, the businessman, for he has no countryman with whom to collaborate. He is a free agent, a man outside who perceives what's going on within. The wild card in the European pack. From what he has told me he has lived an interesting life that has made him wise, patient and strong. A man to admire.

Thoughts disturbed by jangle of keys. A *Functionale* throws a young Nigerian into the cell. He is given the bed next to me. After a while of staring he turns to me.

"Excuse me..." His English is slow and difficult..."Excuse me. I don't mind to die here. But I don't want to suffer, suffer...Always the suffering...."

"No problem" says Bernie the other Englishman, a Geordie. "Have some bread."

The Nigerian cowers. He thinks he will die. His eyes wander in the dim light. He wants the food but he thinks it poisoned. Eventually I take the bread and break it. I take my half and eat. He eats the bread suspiciously and then hungrily.

I discover, in this moment, that sharing bread with a hungry man is indeed a communion. Together you live, together you give. Here, bread is very valuable and in its rarity reveals its pricelessness.

Music plays. Another day disperses. A very odd tea is made. Odd that is compared to Surrey tea, which is drunk in the well made cleanly designed architecture of middle class England. This strange tea consists of mint and lemon.

The Nigerian realises
That he's still alive,
In some sort of jingoist hell.
Bread 'tis broken,
Pains token,
Whispers
Tea and cards

Silently and unnoticed, a silver moonbeam,
Steals into the room.
Another night begins.

The Italians have prepared a feast for everyone. Rice, vegetables, and mint tea. Afterwards we have biscuits and hashish. The best meal I've had since I got here. Everyone partakes. Those with money, those without. As we are all very hungry, this food was eaten with a great deal of respect. Every nationality sat cross legged on the floor. Army began playing his harmonica. The thrill of eating clean food, for the first time in days. In the candlelight I thought of the M.E.C. or E.E.C., as I looked at the shadowy faces around me.

'How Europe could well learn from Ceuta,' ran my mind. 'Here we were together as one nation. French, German, Brits. An alliance of all into communed comrade ship.' I was touched near to vulnerability. One day, when all the tears are cried. ....Peace...Pax...Being as one. The sum total....A vision or hallucination?

'Viva Italiano,' laughed someone.

Awoke, not with the sparkle of communed comradeship, but the memory of again nearly have a fight with Paul the Englishman. Next time he makes some sly comment I shall say nothing and let my fists do the talking. After all, I've got nothing to loose and I can't believe someone can be so blatantly impolite.

'Wind ups' typical of the English. I guess I'm equally culpable in my own way. Just see it easier in others than I do myself.

Morning brings depression especially with overcast skies.
"No sun. No fun, " says Bruno, sensing my vibration.

Yes this day finds me very down. Greyness everywhere. I wonder if anyone will think I'm worth 100,000 pesetas, which I'm reliably informed will be the bail set for my release. Sometimes I wonder. Here I am, one more ostensibly foul place in which to be, and my only excuse is its a good place to write. An itchiness from who knows what, invades my thoughts. It could be caused by the blanket or mattress.

Maybe this whole exercise book is merely a succession of disjointed words which say very little as a whole. They could be nothing more than haphazard paint on canvas, with no overall affect. Maybe I should or could have carried on towards being an academic. All I can say with some certainty is, that no one has attempted the same subject matter as myself, in the same way. I hope I communicate what it is I'm supposed too. A collection of perceptions grasped out of moments met here, in the bowels of the Earth.

'PLEASE TO MEET YOU"

Said the young gentleman,
in this cool evening.
Please to meet you too.
I am life and death. Alpha and Omega; the Beginning and the End; the one which is all
and the All that is One. I am, only what I am. Who are you?
Which face does race
Inside your mind
This Time.
The Beginning?
The End ?
Lost my sunglasses
Smashed lenses
A million sunbursts
Refract through water.

Unbelievably, the English ask me to contribute to their tea boat. Only the English would run a tea boat in Ceuta Prison. Only the English would think of it...Or could.

Two new Germans arrive this afternoon during siesta. Norbert and Rudi caught with eighteen kilos in their petrol tank. Norbert looks worried and lies down staring at the ceiling. Rudi has been given the bed next to me. He is slim, blond haired and blue eyed. He winks at me, smiles and from beneath his overall produces a well concealed hand made pipe, and some superb hashish.
'You wish a pipe?' He asks. I need no second invitation and after two of his concoctions we converse.

In his guttural yet precise English, he vividly described travelling shadowed valleys, on one kidney. He pointed to his right hand side. Rudi was the 26 year old son of a local Police Inspector. He came from Freiberg which is on the edge of the Black Forest. At the age of 20 Rudi went to Art School. Here he became bewitched by a fellow student and they began to get stoned. On his 21st birthday, Rudi and some friends took smack and passed out. Rudi slept for twenty hours on his right side.

"After a while because I have only one kidney," he explained himself precisely, 'the brain told the heart to stop pumping the blood on the right side."
He sunk into a coma. There were others there, people unable to notice his plight. Finally someone tried to wake him, couldn't, and called the hospital.
They had to incise and drain the right arm, which had swollen from drying blood. The whole mechanism of his limb, withered proportionately without liquid. He lost the use of his right arm.

"Afterwards for six weeks I had to drink only pure fresh milk. One litre a day. It became like morphine drinking this milk." He concluded, as if contemplating how the liquid had pulsated life back, into his tired being.

Evening:

The sun has come,
Day 'tis done,
Beat a retreat,
To repeat,
This silently aching heat.
Today,
The sun has come.

Headaches.
Silent smile
Teeth tight
Windless breath,
Meaningless words
Thrown to air,
Sun
Rest now : Be at Peace.
Moon
She's coming soon.
Grey, blue, silver beams,
Sweeping skies.
Surrender day
'Tis nights turn
To burn up dreams.

Chess, early evening Ceuta. I reflect back. The consulate visited me today and took my details. He thinks I'll get bail of 50,000 Pesetas. Still—What will be,—Will be. It will be interesting to see, which way
The Wind blows.
Light bad,
Candle bursting in its final flame
Darkness.

This morning awoke and reflected on seeing myself, in a mirror yesterday. Fine, even growth on week old beard. Strange to look at oneself for the first time in seven days. Wasn't as bad as I thought. Had fantasies about big pock marks, on cheeks.

Morning sun, bright and hot.

Butter, morning drinking chocolate, dog ends, litter by the single draining hole on the *patio.*

I gave a shirt to Rudi the one armed German in exchange for some of his hashish. His partner Norbert was the prime mover in their scam and he wears a furrowed brow. Eighteen kilos in the petrol tank could be a long time. Rudi tells me more of his experience with the Black Out in the Freiberg Commune, when he lost the use of his arm. This was 'the Big Trip' for him. When he eventually recovered, after two weeks in a coma he didn't recognise himself. It was, he said like being born, dying, and being reborn again. A Freak. He says his arm swelled up to the size of his leg. The doctor made an incision and the arm, withered to what it is now.

Imagine it—For Yourself,

How you'd feel,

As the black revulsion,

Seeps from your useless side,

Pulsating out in time

With the tapping heart.

The Rhythm of life.

Eyes glued to your own monstrosity,

Withering,—A/Trophy.

He tells me that sometimes when his one kidney is not so clean, his stubble of an arm feels as if its been caught in a grinding machine.

Hiding in shadows

From sun.

I ask Massimo, an Italian from Rome, for my pen back. He's disappointed to no longer draw his designs. He asks for a cigarette, I give him my last one, half smoked. Laughter. Business at Los Rosales.

There is a fort outside as well as inside. Next door in fact like two terraced houses and its an outpost of The Spanish Legion, '*Lecion*' as they are known here. I had no idea foreign legion still existed in 1979. It shines a brilliant white in afternoon sun and you can espy a sentry or two, like mirages in the deep blue gleaming stratosphere.

Jean Marc is a small Frenchman from near Toulouse. He came here the same day as me and we discuss the merits of St Exupery. He has had a dream, he tells me, about flying free to Marseilles. He soars like Le Petit Prince, far above the prison walls. "Une Reve", from which he fell into the Earth with the air rushing past his body so fast, he couldn't breathe. Then he awoke to the *brigada* of hell.

Canary sings soft tune,
Murmur of Marocs.
Still peace of Siesta time.

They call in Morocco, the dope which is to all intent and purpose the "Tops" or best, 'SPUTNIK'—Take Off, blasted out into the cosmos.—A trip....

Floor lineoed.
Cool " *brigada*",
Talk in five languages
Sunbursts
'Cross prism'd candle holder.

Time here has ceased to be. Watches are valueless. The day is two hundred years ago. Wake Up, sometime between 7 a.m. and 8.30 a.m. Courtyard, *patio* time till 2.00 p.m. 2.30 p.m. to 5.30 p.m. locked up in *brigada*. 5.30 p.m.—8.00 p.m., outside in *patio*/Courtyard. Then *brigada* from 8.00 p.m.—9.30 a.m. Just to prove to myself that time hasn't really ceased to be here, more merely done a personality change in which the figures just quoted are demoted, or promoted, to some other plane or dimension, irrelevant here. As here is irrelevant there. Our time here is not "measured out in coffee spoons. " Our time is measured out by sun, wind, bread, water, hashish, conversation in the four seasons of a Ceuta year.

I write in riddles
Little magic spells
To weave the world.
I write in riddles
Ancient rites, decision,
No room for imprecision.

I have been here long enough to get to know the Spaniards a bit. Force of economics means trying to sell some clothes and they, apparently, are the best hustlers. Courtyard fills with evening shadows. Light fluff of cloud films, scatter heat before one's eyes. Staring into sun refracted through rain bowed prism. Eyes bright with fires reflection. A deflection.

Still, the Nigerian, Sumi, asks at the centre when they are going to kill him. The *Functionales* laugh and raising pretend guns fire. Sumi ducks to avoid an imaginary bullet. Sumi talks to no one. He walks up and down as if he has a heavy mind.—Wanted he trusts no one. His fear is apparent in his body language and he cowers, nostrils flaring with paranoia. All the time he sleeps when we're in the *brigada*. When we're in the Courtyard he eats nothing, fidgets and waits
For the blazing of guns.

The German, Rudi, has a pain in his arm. I look. It is red and inflamed. We talk of life, heroin, the trip. For him, as for me, Ceuta in the sun 'tis "No Problem." Mist forms on mountain top as evening plays a new tune to the world.

Depression. My dream of Marin County, California, seems a long way off. This whole story of my life 'tis just one of failure. My mother no doubt will pay for my release. But then what? I have a feeling that all I'll be left with is this manuscript, in an attempt to finally justify to myself what I am or am not.

A moment, from another world.
Somewhere, wherein,
I belong,
At some point in time and space.
All I have is these stories, paintings of life, a belief in my own experience.

Experience in
Many distant lands,
Strange traces
Of the Mind.

I know not what I say to you, nor need to know. Your space 'tis yours. You need not know what I mean to say to you. My space 'tis mine.
From the window I see the hills, the fort, the first distant strains of electric light. Birds flying in the cool sunset.
Tranquillo.
Ceuta Evening
Play.
Sumi wants to swap bunks with me. No way will I swap. Day turns to night.
Food bad,
Bed too,
Bugs and bees
Down on my knees.
DIRE STRAITS once more on the Radio.

"Ah well another day, another doughnut"—said the sun. Spaniards, intermittently, screech a language of the morning air. Radio Plays. Outside a dumper truck hisses and churns the silence.

I've badly miscalculated, financially, although I guess living on ten pounds for a week isn't too bad. Now I'm broke and distracted by the itching from sleeping between blankets, which are full of who knows what. Living, now, as the pauper. This morning was the first morning, I've not bought coffee from the shop. Feel thoroughly sick of this whole affair of life. Burning, slither of sun slices the *patio* with heat.

I awake. Reconcile myself to flies and heat. To talking pigeon English for communication, and to the itchiness of my beard. Have taken up my pens for another day's toil and am rewarded within minutes.

'You want?' Rudi hands me a tin containing a taste of thick Black Coffee.

The sun has finished me today—It has revealed itself in a stark blind nakedness. White Light/White Heat. My beard itches terribly. I will have it shaved this afternoon, if I can get a few pesetas. Each day I feel more like a caged animal and I look forward more, to that bathe in the cool Mediterranean sea. There are far too many people here. Feel oppressed by overcrowding. Only just beginning to recognise this.
Dirt, Dustbins, Old Cans, Old Boots.
"That foul slut who keeps the till." My mind goes back to my recent university study of Yeats. I dismiss the reminiscence with another angle.

The language problem here is difficult. I speak no Spanish, nor Moroccan. Most conversation conducted in signs, with hand motions replacing words in communication. The Europeans all have a representative linguistic. I speak the best French out of the English and mingle with all the groups.

Feeling like an Ambassador
Pen sweeps thru' pages
Word flow.
Each morning
Get up
Take pen
Paper
Lines of rhymes
To Write.

'Tis a strange feeling watching foreigners converse in another language. It is like watching a dance, for one searches the movement for expression.

You see what you see and you hear what you hear, the result of this solution your perception. Your own interpretation of a Nation.

Siesta time approaches
Hair thick with midday sweat
Each time
I look at
The last word written
Thought races
Pacing through my madness
To the next sign
On the next line.

Siesta time 'tis slow. Sumi, sits on my bed, head in hands, dreaming of the guns. He fears his time has come. All round the bottom of his splayed nose are tiny white spots. He lives alone, despairing not knowing what to do. I wonder what his crime is. He has spoken to me in English, but it seems garbled his belief that his legs and arms will remain in Ceuta, while his spirit will return to Enugu. Maybe he is a refugee. He has no trust or hope in fate.

They are building a larger outer wall here 'cos some people tried to escape. Others plan it.....Desperadoes.....I doubt they will in reality.

Slow melodic afternoon. Soft voices. French 'scamming' their next deal by the map. Dry mouth. Bed harsh. Rudi with one kidney groans himself to sleep. Silence .

Moroccan Music on very tiny radio. Sun makes a right angled space of light in the Western corner of the *patio*. Trying to sell my Wrangler Jeans for 300 Pesetas i.e. Packet of Cigarettes and a few cups of coffee. During siesta this afternoon I make a bracelet of coloured beads for myself and Rudi. Maybe when the Spanish middle man returns I will have a shave, to celebrate my failure.

Have to drop price to 200 Pesetas. Little wispy breeze. Perhaps, I make the deal. I watch The Spaniard looking desperately for a buyer. I am desperate for the taste of blonde nicotine and sweet black coffee, to quench the desert thirst. Flies play, in and out of shadows. The Spaniard has disappeared back to Moroccan corner, I hope its a good sign. I wait for his return.

Here in the shadows is a peace from the furnace that lies no more than 3 foot away. Return of Spaniard still with jeans—A failure. Now I will sulk about having no money.

Got myself a cup of coffee and two 'Blond' cigarettes, so not too bad. Just be nice to have something of one's own. A spare moment alone without humans agitating the background....

Evening,
Whistle,
Time to return.

Day 'tis done.
Cool evening air
Far off mountain top weeps wandering patches of mist.

I think of you;
I have laid my life in your hands
And you have brought me Roses
At sunlight,
Blue moonbeams,
Crystal dreams.
I think of you
With each breath of life,
I breathe.
Night break,
Tranquillo time.

Darkness comes quickly here. As soon as the ball of fire blazes onto the far side of the hill, skies deepen, redden, mellow—soon the ice-cool electricity of evening will sweep the room and outside will tinge and grey with the moon.

Another morning. Slept better last night than I have for the past two days. I laid out flat on the bed using a towel as a blanket, (at least I know its semi clean).

Watched the sunset last night. The two mountains in the distance were the only disturbance to a sky created turmoil. Light-blue, thick bank of greyness that fades to mist round zenith of hills. Blue shades, white sailing boats of cloud. Sky mellows, sun descends, mountain shivers, in final shimmering moment of day.

I would like
To paint sunset

Capture its colour and essence
For a moment glimpse
A sun setting Rainbow.

Sumi seems more peaceful. I guess he's got some sort of equilibrium arising from not being shot at dawn. He should have, after all he's still alive and suffering. Joseph the Russian has cut out a picture which depicts a clear blue sky background to a long black rose. The caption reads "BLACK IS SOUGHT EVERYWHERE." Not only as a black rose, but also as a race of being blacks appear to be sought, like Sumi the Nigerian. Sought after eyes, the dream of freedom turned to the gleam of the hunted as he sits out another Ceuta sunshine day. In some ways drug addicts are the new persecuted, "sought everywhere," by friend and foe alike.

Boredom. Routine. Breakfast. Sunburn. Lunch. Sunburn. Siesta. Evening Sunburn. Night-life. Routine day to day stuff. Drone of home generated power, pitter patters the moment. Waiting for the next movie, in the long hot intermission of this no-mans land.

One of the Spaniards dressed in red shirt and blue jeans cries out from the shadows. The shrill scream cuts the air calling on ones attention. He crouches, squats face covered by hands. For what does he hold his head in horror? Perhaps he wishes to return to the legion. To make amends for the shame he brings to the system and his family.

Or maybe, he wishes to be left alone
To silently weep his tears,
Without the noisy hum drum
Of compatriots lulling him with sympathy—

Why does he cry?—Only he, staring into invisibility, knows the secret of his eyes secretions, of his unknowing pains. Whistle blows. Evening count up time.

Yes! The indefatigable Spaniard whom I call Tweedledum has sold my jeans for 170 pesetas! He smiles triumphantly as he orders his side kick, (Tweedledee), to hand over the money. Tweedledee is reluctant. He has a slight limp and very ragged attire. Tweedledum, the brains of the duo, has one eye missing. They hand me the cash and slope off talking excitedly. At least I've finally got a little money. Enough for coffee and 'blonde' cigarettes. Been here for nine days now. Weather overcast. Making bead bracelets in shadows. Later on the sun will reveal itself again.

Got a big bite on my leg from an insect which has severely swollen my knee. Sound of men making trinkets. Most people gone to the school room to read. I find the small confined space terrible and so I sit on in sun.

Mind wandering back. I thinking about Oxford. I wonder about Brian and Francis my compatriots from the rehabilitation centre with whom I shared a house in Botley after our 'cures.' I dream about the river running by Henry Road. I think about missed college "Balls." About Boxhill and Dorking. The burst of summer colour across the landscape. Mother and Father walking the dog across Deepdene cricket fields. Twilight years in the heart of England. Hypothesis and supposition scratch the page;
As sun peeps out from cloud.....

Rudi the "SPUTNIK" German has run out of "SPUTNIK"—What a few days!!—High on the hashish—I think, maybe my Deborah and Clare shirt will pass on to him. It is ideal, for someone with a withered arm and one kidney, for not only is it cool but also it flows freely, away from the skin. This may aid his sensitive side. He has, he tells me no family except for a "Gut Woman" who is six months pregnant. He lives in Freiberg, near the Black Forest on the border of Germany and Switzerland. He is poor but "rich inside"—I can identify strongly with him, although my freakishness is not as physically apparent as his own. Inside I have travelled similar lands to him.

He wanders across the courtyard,
Thinking of Death.
Sees pulsation in the arm joint, by my left vein.
Points, at his left eye smiles, says—"Hungry,
The Blood is hungry"—He winks
Knowingly.

From out of nowhere a voice shouts "Rainbow. *Regarde-la* "
Regard. Around the sun, in a perfect circle stretching no doubt many miles is the aura of heat, horizoned by a rainbowed halo. An eclipse of distinction.

Shit!—What have I done? Emotion, full of nightly remorse. English still planning their useless scamming. Dull murmurs of late evening conversations. Write.....Write.....Write you bastard!—Spit out the sour taste of man's world in hundreds of millions of words. COMMUNICATE—Yet in whose language, in whose hands, in whose soul? The German Legionnaire, awaiting deportation has had his head shaved. He sits like Buddha, cross-legged on the floor. Despondency, remorse, disillusion seem to be cemented. Where to after Ceuta?.....Some other jail. Some other town. Some other country; Running, running, running on.

I have an ache inside,
Trying to find a home
With no home to go too.

Melodic Neil Young on the Radio. I want to curl up warm by the firelight of my teens, listening to wind blow, and feel secure.

I want to curl up somewhere
and cry my eyes out.
I watch instead the French playing cards. It takes me back.

I can remember only a few occasions as a child when as a family we all sat down to play cards. I think I was a little frightened of my father who had set standards by which he abided and I abused. He stood for the system and I opposed him. Long hair. Going out late. He lived, then, half in the early nineteenth century and half in the present. Desperately attempting to comprehend his son, who lived in a world alien to him.

My father, I believe, has in his own lifetime come very close to God. He has allowed himself to be taught and has, in the face of all adversity maintained these teachings, whilst always being open to changes. I have pained him with my rebelliousness, but he has watched, listened, and perceived. Now he looks back, retrospectively, with the clarity of twilight skies at sunset.

My mother, too, has striven in life. She has striven to give the stability she lacked in her own childhood. Like thousands of other war-torn Jews she ran, like myself, from persecution 'cos other men or women, felt they had the right to judge others of their own species.

We are ALL brothers and sisters,
Originally we all originate
From the same original origin.
The One that became Three
The Three that became One.
Darwin, The Bible, Big Bang,
Whatever theory.
We have no right, as a whole to persecute a part of that whole, because we cannot comprehend that part.
Without that part, our part could not be.
No Black, no White,
"You can't have one without the other".

My Mother dreamed about her eldest son. He would be a man amongst men. For her, in whose belly he lay, each tiny movement he made, was perceived. Before her lay dreams of peace. When he was born he came out all wrong. Head where feet should be. Feet where head should be. Top pointed in some Shakespearean guise. All night he cried, like a tiny kitten. He had no desire to re-enter life. Crying for the warmth of the womb. To be again the seed.

My Mother, through all the pains which she has borne, still stands strong. She knows, as light fades, that indeed her eldest son is a man amongst men. Yet never in her wildest dreams, did she perceive that mare of the night, that spun the future for her loved ones.

If I'd kept every article of clothing that had meant anything to me during the past ten years, I would be a rich man indeed, as far as wardrobes are concerned. Instead, I have sold, lost, had stolen, given away almost everything. Scattered by four winds, they roam the earth attired by other being. An apparition of their former selves, except in that a little part of myself is always with them.

Strange days; Strange ways,
In more ways then one.

What can I say?
Clump of trees.
Fort,
Mountain.
Puff of dust in wind
White buildings, deep-blue sky.
View from a prison window.

Sumi, despite all I tell him, is still convinced he will die here. He will return home in spirit to Nigeria to be born again he tells me. However his head and legs he will leave here in Ceuta for his crimes. Paranoically, he shares coke and biscuits with Rudi and myself. He seems cursed by some insane *ju-ju*—Like myself

In the hands
Of other being.
His eyes seem to know already his fate.
Strangely, strange
Oddly normal.

To get a drink here demands some ingenuity. You find, or preferably buy a full can of coke or fanta. You take the empty tin can and ground it on the granite. After some hours the top breaks in. You remove it and for 10 pesetas can buy a half filled can of coffee! All day there is this sound of metal grinding on granite. Those who cannot afford to visit the tiny hole in the wall they call a *kiosko* must find a can for making even cups for water. Light film of cloud makes evening sun chill. Foreign tongues, anxiety. Spoons and ground down coke cans keeping people alive.

Sumi is certainly spooked. When he gave us biscuits this afternoon it was as if he were a child offering sweets to grown ups. When we accepted graciously his eyes lit up with innocence. I guess he is full of vagueness, terror, and demons. On the one hand he wants to live. But on the other, he wants to forego suffering and life is, to him, suffering. What a dichotomy. Live and suffer or die and be free?.....Perhaps.....

Evening shadow settles. Wondering about persons here, and faraway. I feel in transit. Waiting. The faces here mere stories. Reflections. Characters in a play. An elongated waiting room scene whilst changing trains.....

"If you miss this one," sings the Radio,
"You'll never get another one...
"Last train to San Fernando....."

And faraway. No real lovers. just memories, painting, dreams, imaginings. I wonder what they do, now, as I write these characters faraway yet close at hand.

An argument between Paul, the Englishman I've nearly fought on two occasions and Bruno, the Italian, who controls the electricity. Bruno can't understand how the English can drink so much milky tea and need him to boil water. Bruno boils water by sticking two electrodes in a bowl of water and attaching it to a naked light socket. The English try and explain tea's necessity to the digestive system. Bruno, with increasing verbosity, indicates they use too much of his electricity. The argument heats up. Tempers flare. Another face appears on Bruno—another character evolving from the Ceuta womb. Paul backs off.

Each day I experience some feeling of doubt. Some nagging in my stomach or head that the direction, the space to now, has perhaps been a diversion, an inflection. Once more I must pack my bags and seek another road to travel along.

Fort lights seem miles away. Real stomach ache tonight. Wind is up. Banging windows. My kidneys ache. Three 'Fiesta days. Today, tomorrow, the day after and so no chance of any letters. The wind's up. It blows between the bars and landing, whistling through the cracks. French continue scamming in the corner. Planning intently.

The winds up,
Something in the air.
An aching arsehole
From strange toilets.
Cold floors
A bed bugged bed...

Wind blow on
The way you blow.

Today paper stares blankly. No patterns between lines to create a flow with, just the hazy whim of last night's thoughts returning, with day and my own awakening.

I seem to be casting my mind back lately. I guess 'cos of the lack of incentive and inspiration in the routine here. I think of two of the women I met at the Rehabilitation centre.

Antonia Trentham, Julie Symonds Where are you now?
You whose thick thighs tempted me,
Both of you overvalued your cunts.
They were never the real object of my desires.
I wanted to know, only,
What lay inside your minds;
Now, perhaps,
You mourn me.
For my social failings,
My lack of aspirations,
Yet sometimes,
Alone,
Drinking your wine,
There will be time for you,
To quietly contemplate your envies.

I contemplate, momentarily, their pouting lips which matched those other concealed lips, clenched tightly between their thighs, unable to mouth a word.

One of the legionnaires has a pet thrush that plays in the debris by the water tap. This deserter spends all his time catching flies to feed it. Sleepy day. Jean Marc and his friend have had visits this morning. They seem in high spirits. Got off, no doubt, on knowing that someone remembered them. For me spirits low. Going up and down like a yo-yo. I guess one of the main reasons is that I am done financially. I have not a penny, nor a peseta, to my name. Mind wandering into survival dimension.

When out of nowhere, totally unexpected, Jean Marc puts 50 pesetas in my hand.

Sun hot. Impossible to describe skies activity as I sit on the fiery granite bench. Voices murmuring, strange tongues.

I remember back to Antonia Trentham. The last time we met. Late one night, in the shadows, you seeing me in the street and kissing me, telling me you'd left the rehabilitation centre yourself for a life of market trading and 'group therapy.' I, by then, as you knew, had already un rehabilitated myself and was travelling already the road that leads here. Your face smiling and I, hoping for understanding, in your eyes.

And, you, Julie Symonds, with your dark gypsy eyes and those large flushed fulsome breasts you once let me fondle for a mere thrill, in our non sexual non addict able world.

This life 'tis as a dream. Anything outside the moment a fantasy. Irrelevant in many respects, to this world of waiting and anticipating the next movie.....Yet I make few plans for the future, nothing more than ideas waiting to flower if the money comes. If I have the allies, the backing.

Where are you now Antonia Trentham and Julie Symonds?
Basking in sunshine, tripping the light fandango
Or playing a game played out, before this time,

Dreaming of new tomorrows
Living on borrowed ideas
And Yesterday's fear?
Where are you now Antonia Trentham and Julie Symonds?
I wanted to know, only,
What lay inside your mind
When sometimes alone, drinking your wine,
You had the time
To quietly contemplate your envies.

Siesta. Wind blows, tea, hashish, "chocolate". Some Moroccans have stolen one of my shirts. If I see someone wearing it I shall attack them. French still playing cards. English still planning the biggest cannabis deal in known history. An afternoon of hazy heat passing onward. I wonder how Brian is, 'cos he really got caught in the slipstream of my last two weeks at Oxford. Still maybe he learnt more from my maelstrom than his rehabilitation.
Past people from another time,
Flowing into the moment.

Rushing to the present, whilst the chatter of the living thrashes the air. I look at the faces. Army, the Buddhist German murder. Aldo, an unfortunate German junkie and Max his Italian Equivalent. Rudi, one kidneyed German "SPUTNIK". Sumi staring at the ceiling. The murmur of the British now talking politics. The French "Jouent a carte" and myself, writing, not quite sure why, what, or wherefore, all this be. Ceuta, Los Rosales.— Memories and dreams at siesta. Pen gliding through paper.

Black crow appears in sky, hovers before face of sun. Head and beak glisten in golden rays. Solitary, noble, disdainfully it stares down at the Earth, circles and then disappears into nowhere, leaving the *patio* to the naked glare of day.

Slept late into the afternoon. When I got out to the *patio*, the area of sun was a small triangle in the eastern reflection. Shadows lengthening. The food was really disgusting this evening. A broth with insects. The Germans play war games. Pink Floyd play on radio. Bad cold staved off by Bruno's herbal medicines. Drugged feverish imaginings.

Coincidentally I saw, today, in an old newspaper, the story of a girl I knew. Being the sister of a famed actress, she spoke of the horror of her drug addicted situation. Judy mentioned to me she'd sold her story for five thousand pounds. She didn't mention what I remembered. The flight that dawn in her Mercedes across Hammersmith Bridge. She mentioned nothing of our meeting, nor its sunburst; nor that whole dimension. She talked of self degradation—

She told what she knew they wanted to know.
When I had seen another side.
Eyes—Never have I seen such eyes;
Hair—Never have I seen such hair.
Stars for eyes; Fairies weave her braids.
I have seen a little piece of her in every woman.
Who are you?—
Goddess that haunts me;
Helen of Troy; Cleopatra; Boadicea; or all these and more ?

The tale of Medusa is one that has always fascinated me. Medusa I believe was the woman with the most beautifully hypnotic voice, yet a face so terrible it turned you to stone if you saw it, when tempted by her plea, for you to face her.
'Tis not her ugliness, but her beauty that turns him to stone. In perceiving all woman, no one woman may satisfy that man who has perceived her, who is all woman—All men at some moment glimpse her in some form of orgasm—But for those whom she chooses to haunt, 'tis the horror of living with the memory of your meeting with beauty, that turns you to stone.

Antonia Trentham, Julie Symonds, where are you now ?
Suburbanized, forgotten
Dreary dead lead worried about how fat you are
Or have you found out, the reason,
For the season your in
And let her,
Enter you........

No breakfast today for several reasons. When I went to take my stale bread out to the *patio* my way is stopped by a broad *Functionale*. He lets me know that if I want to eat I must stay in the dining area. On receiving this information my eyes look down at the roll of stale white bread passing as breakfast. It is crawling with tiny white maggots. I feel sick put my cup of warm water on the table, slamming the plate defiantly on the floor. Straight backed I turn to exit. I don't get far. The butt of a gun slows me down and I am grabbed, thrown to the ground and punched by three burly guards. They quickly haul me off dragging my body by my hair over the granite *patio* and down a flight of stairs. I am thrown aching, into a cell with one electric light bulb. My scalp pounds and tufts of hair come away in my hands. The swinging bulb foretells torture. Two of the guards return. They hold my arms while an officer slaps my face and punches my body incessantly for about 30 seconds. It all seemed unreal.

"This nota Englande. This Espagne...." Echoes each blow.

"Pardona..." I beseech him.

When I reach the point of near collapse they pour water on me and take me back to the *patio*. Humiliated.

What a freak out!!—Sky overcast. Unlike the Spaniard yesterday I sneak off to the open toilet where flies thrive round the human wastage. Tears for myself. Wanting only to be alone. God! This life is heavy for me. A succession of ugliness in which to perceive beauty. Someone, somewhere is laughing. Baton charge. War of man on man. Ridiculousness.

My fault, I guess after the tears subside, and I realise they're not going to come back and give me a second going over. Maybe I was far too over confident and arrogant. Jaw aches, foot scratched. Most people wandering aimlessly now.

They could kill you here and no one would know anything about it. Men in green uniforms, parading corpses at dinner time. Just a flicker of sun; a faint trickle of hope. Hungry always hungry, bromide in everything, no sexual drive. Spaniards play *Ludo*. I itch from bedbugs. Foot hurt from scratch. Scalp, face, and body ache dully now. Tired and weak.

The pain of life is living. All who live have pain. You may be led to believe that there is some Nirvana here on this world but if you do you are fooling yourself. There is no peace or contentment which lasts. Peace and contentment come only in moments and then fly on elsewhere. Equality, liberty, democracy—socialist or conservative—are myths. Blinkers to limit the sight.

We all have life and life only. We must utilise it. Learn from as many experiences as is possible, in order to fill our beings with information for the next moment.

Stomach ache bad. Could be the beatings or could well be hunger pains. Sun appears for only a few seconds. Realise how utterly alone I am here. At least 1500 miles from my homeland, aching and sad. A sensation impossible to really communicate . The Spanish equivalent of a trustee throws water in the rubbish bin and pours the swill into the drainage hole. Water runs from leaking tap. Remnants of dreams trickling into the rubbish heap.

The best moments of the day have been my breakfast on the *patio*, sitting on the tarmac, bread in mouth and hand. Now these moments are finished—Relegated to the dining-room with the dirt and manners of this particular Hacienda.

Senseless people, eyes fired with insanity
Sounds that spew from cracked lips
Dust of generations swirling in moonshine
The winds of time blown to the four corners
Of the world.

Bernie, the reasonable Geordie Englishman, has left today. His Bail of 200,000. pesetas paid and he's walking the streets again. Another of the English had a letter in which they said that Maggie Thatcher has decided to outlaw unions and bring back conscription for everyone under 27. I guess it'll help the potential unemployment problem, but how popular a measure? Time tells all tales, and anyway I can't see it being a definite proposition already.

On the door of the *brigada* is a painting of the jungle. A swaying branch breaks the suns glare on water.

Depression, the English here seem to think that they are smugglers and the only good person is another smuggler. They mock my words and my efforts with them. They are right, I guess, 28 years old. Nothing published. All I have is self belief to run on. Nose aches from morning beating.

Patchy sort of day. Half blue, half grey. The evening part is the best for me. Day being almost over, turned downhill, body and mind easing with thoughts of sleep. Too much bread has constipated me I think. MIMI MAMASS graffitti'd on the wall here. Now, carrion birds break shrilly the sound of silence.

What a day. Beaten up, run down, yet still high. Joseph, the Russian, smoking a cigar sits on his bed staring at every one here. Everyone goes to talk with him, for he speaks everyone's language fluently, so silently he may listen, staring occasionally to the far mountains with a sad, weary look. His hair greys at the edges, like the hilltops surrounded by evening mist. His clothes are tatty; he has, or looks as if he has, no money, no dreams, no past, no future; only his futile passage through time.

Rolling Stones on cassette. Nose and scalp still ache from morning beating. Dragged across floor by "screws," taken to a little room, where I am slapped and punched . At one point in time, a baton appeared but it was not included in the punishment. The first slap really stung, those that followed fell on numbed face and body. Sordid panic in pit of stomach. Shock. Fear. An animal caged in with superiors, overpowered by physical pain.

No rules here
'Cept the rule of the jungle
Law of pain
All those under 27 take up your gun and learn to kill.

The door opens. It is the Red Band/Trustee. He comes to lock up some of the Italians who work in the kitchen. He looks like Quasimodo. He has one eye semi-poked out, hanging from its socket. He is badly hunchbacked and pockmarked. His clubbed foot sounds unique, as he drags it down the bare, echoing corridor. An evening observation, on a man who sweats out the slime of porous being. His mouth, has a smattering of gold teeth, and half a tongue with an excess of spittle. He smiles as his key turns the lock on another day.

26 people in a small room. Never out of each others sight. No space for a quiet wank. How much do people get on each others nerves? Every person here develops for themselves their own piece of space. A small prism within the prison of their lives. Some oddity which they keep locked inside their hearts. A little diamond to treasure during dream time.

In order to survive
And stay alive
One brief moment, totally alone, feeling the space fly to me.

One brief moment with myself, before having to turn into a chameleon in order to satisfy others.

A new day. Sun is up. Swifts play in air pockets, gliding cross unbroken blue sky. My paper dilapidates with all the folding. Scalp still aching. Shook the fleas out of my blankets today in the early morning half light, making dust everywhere. All of us mumbling our tired strained voices to another Ceuta day.

CLEAN. A cold shower, hair washed, fresh clothes. The sun itself appears brighter after such a gift. The morning strangely quiet. Half the prisoners are showering; and us who have received this luxury stare into bare brightness, play chess, cards, read books, or wash clothing.

Tranquillo.
Searching for a theme
Some dream
of consistency.

Push, push, push myself, keep flowing through the mire of being. Let it come out like drainage to the sea; like the sperm seed to the womb egg. Flow, flow, flow, let the words keep moving, soothing the aches and pains of life.

Whitewashed walls. Thin slithers of dirt splayed across virginity. Dankness and damp seeping through to the senses. Keep writing. Keep CLEAN.

With some people language is totally international. Communication is made through eyes and gestures. I don't know whether many people, actually pick up what another person is transmuting through words. I am sure that whilst one person is talking, on many occasions, the listener hears only his own thoughts. The real communication takes place outside the realms of words. It occurs in the flicker of an eye lid. The mating of two flies. The sounds outside the talk, and the sights within the circle of the eye. Two Spaniards, fearfully destroy a wasp. In the shadow of my 'jeans knee' two flies carry on—Fucking.

Tweedledum dips my pocket for a comb. I challenge him to return it menacingly. After yesterday, I'm really angry my eyes blazing. He tries to turn it into a joke by pretending to give it to me and then, at the last second, snatching it away. The anger wells up in me. Eventually I manage to grab his finger and cling on, twisting it back. He returns the comb. A battle won. Bruno mediates a treaty between us. Really I like Tweedledum, the Catalonian. He is a lonely, poor man, who wanders the courtyard shoeless and wearing only shorts. He comes from Barcelona, living with pestilence all his life, running down the mean streets, taking what he can, when he can. His eyes are darting, always looking for an opportunity. Apparently he is a deserter from the Legion and I find it hard to visualise this person, sweating in Army uniform. His gun at his side, living in a desert fort, immaculately dressed, till he knew that there was nothing worse than an ocean of sand and so he absconded, seeking only peace in his despair. Now he is here at Ceuta, passing time, amusing himself by stealing from Europeans.

In order to stay alive

Tattooed arms; broken shoes;

Can't read no news.

Broken feet walk over broken glass,

Torn to shreds

A silver head

A silent scheme

An undreamt dream.

Tweedledum is berated by his friend, Tweedledee who is smaller but more nattily dressed. He brought a pair of shoes from me. Bruno, the Italian Treaty maker pulls the skin down at the bottom of his eye, points at the pair and smilingly says:-

"Fox and cat".....An apt description.

Massimo and Mario, two of the Italians that I get on well with, are being let out. They were called out to the Centre a minute ago and now have gone to collect their things. Maybe I'll see them again, some other time some other space. Our relationship has been short and intense. Memories of moments to be stored.

They both had jobs. Wondering if maybe I should take a job here in the kitchens? I guess my experience working at the Pizza Parlour would be very valuable, in running a kitchen on a low budget, and also it might.....

"One day they will cover us all..." Interrupts Joseph the Russian." Under what?...I don't know, Mountains, Sea, or Sand it will be that way for all peoples....." Glint of creases round shadowed eyes. A picture of a black rose, swaying in the wind.
'Well,' continues my thought, ' it might be valuable 'cos it would enhance my culinary abilities. An asset any where. Also through working you can buy your freedom.'

Someone dying in the distances.
Someone up against the wall.
Someone crying out in instances.
Someone sighing in the fall.

The only real revolutionaries are the freaks.—"Blessed are all "freaks" for they shall inherit the earth." Socialism, bureaucracy, capitalism, multinational corporations, the military, pluralism, democracy, fascism, the list 'tis infinite. Whatever politics purports to the kingdom, whatever socio-political economic structure exists, in whatever state you be, Marxism knew nothing of Marijuana, nor Space/Time equations, nor L.S.D. Life is always ahead of the academics by about 200 years. - Nature's answer to the mechanisation of man by man has been to produce a species of "freaks;" abnormals; insanes; physically and mentally she has chosen a Band of Gypsies. A sigh in the wind; caricatures, dwarfs, monstrosities; or merely oddities of a kind, undefined.—Found in faery-land, outside the norm.....

Sgt Peppers Lonely Hearts Club Band.
Roaming, cloaked and disguised 'cross the cosmic.

Flies, lives, wives, old school ties; blood red trail of sunset. Shiver of crystal, shimmer of heat. Sad when Massimo and Mario went. Guess relationships here will be strong. After all everyone here, more or less, has committed the same crime—"TURNING ON"—In sharing the same crime, we harden through unison, belief in each and everyone's ability To make it through the night.

'Cos everyone, everywhere in the world, is a little bit of a "freak".

 Taffy the Welshman walks round and round the *patio*, on and on he travels, as if he must get to work on time. I wonder about his family, whether he's still with his wife or maybe they're divorced. I know he has a son. Round and round he travels. A circular spin on the roundabout of time.

Evening chill. Light breeze curls paper. Cold reflection in dirty pool of leaking water. Tap of spoon on granite, chairs being moved. Spanish slowly chat. More walkers; more travellers on the roundabout. Whistle blows three times for end of day.....
The world spins round; Autumn, Winter, Spring, Summer.

A circle.
Inside the circle
A triangle.
A triangular circle!?!
A Cyclical triangle!?!

A moments travel may be as such.....No need for feet, no need for body. Travel through perpetually changing time and space, is being. Being is the experience of your own particular voyage through perpetually changing time and space.

Sands sifting through the hour glass of life,
Each grain—A moment
As is the sun sum total of all grains.....

Neil Young on Tape Recorder. Still in prison. No letters, no telegrams, no visits. Oh woe is me!! French play cards. Sumi my Nigerian mate is no longer in the throws of death; perked up, speaks and plays. Chess, tea, evening activities—'Tis odd really I've come here to write and actually put my money where my mouth is and written.—"Heelo Mistah Robins, writing de book"—says an Italian walking by—
Guess he's right. I am actually writing a book.

A rotund Frenchman who wears pyjamas sits on his bed playing a very good harmonica "Blues for the Loire Valley". Evening time. Sleepy heads. Only the French remain awake playing their card-game incessantly—Cool peaceful end of day feeling. "Another day; Another Doughnut"—An idiom. A saying.

Today I start working as a cleaner in the "*brigada*". Bruno got me the job, its quite easy really and above all peaceful. Awfully difficult living with twenty six others so to spend an hour sweeping the floor, when they've all gone is really unwinding. Time to turn around, and know nobody watches you.
Don't hustle me today Espana.
Don't knock me off my feet.
Feeling run down, a joker, a clown.
Lump on my ear, I'm wearing a frown.
Don't hustle me today Espana,
Your Roses smell pure,
Los Rosales the cure,
In the heat of some long distant down.

No new people for quite sometime. Last night there was a fight in the Spanish *brigada* over thieving. Lots of shouting and horrible, blood curling screams. The rush of guards. Apparently one man has had his wrists slashed and may not survive.

Blood spurting to Earth

Like water in the *patio*

Pumps its way to drainage

Rusty floor, sucks in life blood of man.

I wonder if readers of this fairy-tale, this reality, this composition, book or poem will find it heavy going? For a moment stop and think as if this is the end of the story and recapitulate over what you've already read. Has it been heavy going?—Has it been light, humorous, ugly or beautiful? Think about it.... Maybe light a cigarette or joint and look round you.....Then remember you've still got further to go, not only in terms of reading, but also in life.....

Lazy Sunday afternoon—Cards with the French. Joan Baez on the cassette singing— "With God on Our Side". I remember hearing this record as a 15 year old.—Really said something meaningful to me in a world which, at that time, appeared to be becoming increasingly meaningless.

Two French brothers arrive, Jean and Jacques. They did a run together and got busted with 40 kilos. I try to imagine how I'd feel if my brother Jeremy was here. For me it would be a great advantage, but the end as far as Mum and Dad are concerned. I would be totally ostracised, thrown out, an outcast. Maybe it'll be that way anyway. Possibly I'll be left here, friendless, to fend for myself through these hot afternoons. Possibly, but I believe someone will save me!!

Writing tired, uninspired, boredom of monotony. Continuously similar existence. Day to day. Time totally different here. A different gauge of being. Day/Night—Night/Day—All in one—One in All—An elongated period of time in a world incomprehensible to all those who make conjecture as to what that world is like. Unless you live it—You don't know it.

Everyone in their own way is doing time—

Life is time—Time is life—Without time there would be no movement and life as we know it would cease to be.

Sad indeed.

Blue sky, an oceanic demarcation to the end of this particular planets space and the beginning of some other space. Filter of light through barred windows. Striking of match. Wide-eyed stares—Chocolate coloured dreams.

Maybe, it has been this way for many men. Solitary, slow, an internal, rather than an external exploration. Cowboys on Ranches; Wandering bands of Arabs—Lawrence of Arabia—Men who left ships at strange unknown ports, never to return. Searchers, "Hombres;" Seekers after that which has never been before—Alchemists of the mind weaving the human line through the winds of fate. Romantic thoughts, and visions passing by the window like fluffs of clouds. Pen gliding now—words, words, words, spewing out from a hammered brain drained by the lottery of life.

I wanted really to write a novel. Something gripping, that would set peoples adrenaline running with excitement. They would have to turn the pages nervously 'cos they'd be in such a hurry to read the final, ultimate, climax.—But then you put the book down, and it becomes nothing more than something that has been and gone, demanding little comprehension.

I belong to a rare species of poets, philosophers, dreamers. Our writing demands your consistent attention. Each syllable contributes to the making of the whole. We demand your comprehension too, in order to perceive from a similar angle to our own.—Breeze, soft, sullen. Batons splayed acrobatically in air, by out of office legionnaires. I get up, take a walk into sunlight.

My relationship with the German "SPUTNIK" (Rudi) has developed well. We work a crazy business dealing in Western Clothing. Odd how people meet and automatically 'click'—Relationships that are meant to be. 'Tis 'cos we have travelled similar roads in life's journey and read the signs in similar ways. Ripples and bubbles scuttle into drainage....

Rudi, Bruno, myself, make magic at evening time. We have a ring each which will go into pawn. Mine is the one that Judy gave to me. I have thought about this giving away of all that remains, physically, of her.

I have memories, Judy, of strange unending nights that turned unnoticed into day and back to night again. You and I the only two constant stars in a revolving universe. I have memories, of almost every moment I had with you and can take anyone, back in time with me, as I relive every minute detail of an experience with you. You, no doubt, also can take people on a magic carpet ride of our mutual living.

More valuable than diamond rings
Rarer than all material things
Finer than a gentle swing
Of dust in wind.
More mellow than a bird that sings,
The Rain bowed prism
Of your heart.

Anyway when I called you were out but in my mind. And I came 1,000 miles to see you.....

Rudi told the Gold Dealer, who was showing off his flash watch, that here, at Los Rosales a watch was meaningless. Rudi is correct but the Moroccan looked as if he'd taken offence. I kick Rudi lightly, in order that he comprehends. He comprehends and explains that we are criticising the concept of time, rather than the aesthetic quality of his very beautiful and expensive chronometer. The Gold Dealer's pride is restored. Day continues, winding its way towards the mountain and then, as it falls beneath the hills heights, lets night in through the back door.

Bruno beckons me with a whistle. I go over and he shows me a picture—A snake curled double, round a stick placed below an advert for Schweppes. The two intermingle together well in some strange way, as does the picture of a Rolls Royce placed on top of the previous two. "Is good?" he says....and laughs.

Utterly miserable today, not even enough pesetas to get any coffee. Mouth tarred by black tobacco. Another morning in the concrete *patio* listening to languages mumbled in alien tongues. Whistle blows, feel really angry want just to be alone. What a life!—Lost for words, waiting in the wings for hope.

The large, jolly Frenchman, caught with a chess set made of hashish crouches in the corner of the courtyard . Crying. Wind cold, sniffing with the icy chill blown earthward from the mountain. Why does he cry this archetypal Frenchman with the big stomach and infectious laugh?—What news has destroyed him?—Turned him into pain?—Maybe his wife has left him—or maybe he can no longer play the role of his smiling facade and lets trickle down his face, water from his heart.

Dirty day enough rubbish on the floor here at the "Restaurant" to make the sweepings of a street. Watching Rudi play chess with another German as day winds its way towards lunch.....

Perhaps the Frenchman, who now stares despairingly into space, sees only broken dreams scattered in the dirt. His wife, I'm told, will divorce him and he is to lose his job.— Connections with the past broken, the first pangs—of Death.....

Talk with fellow Englishman about various things, good to talk for a while, but know that it's a conversation which can't really develop. He asks me, and I ask him, to solve problems that concern another world in which we have no real idea as to how the other lives. Fruitless. I tell him that life up to going into prison can be regarded as a literary sentence, with one's entry into prison a full stop, to that sentence. One's period in prison is like life, (in brackets), and on one's release one begins, a new sentence!!—An interesting analogy.

The Frenchman continues to be perturbed. He walks sullenly up and down the *brigada*, head held low. Sometimes he stops, sits on bed, head in hands, finding out what its like to be made into a desperado.

I think my letters will reach England today. Speculate on the outcome. The surprise or lack of surprise. The possible ostracising of myself from my family. Their fears, like the drips of water in the *patio*. Mother's tears, father's disillusion. Brother's comprehension. My hopelessness, my dreams, dashed on the rocks.....

I'm sorry, I was born to cause you so much pain. But my life has never been one of self-deception and I have always accepted my fate. As Einstein says—"God casts the die—Not the dice".....

There is no life nor death; in terms of finalities. There are many stars, many worlds to learn about; to perceive. Through eternity we travel and experience. We have all, everyone of us been space/being since the time beginnings began, voyaging through the cosmos until we find our way back home. The planet earth itself is part of the Christian Heaven/Hell realm, but we may lay aside now such dreams. We have come 2,000 years from then and have aged beyond such myths.—You, reader, don't believe me, but you will in the moment of death as you reach out for her hands to take you to new lands.

Clothes lying in semi-sunshine waiting to dry. Breeze rustles them. Clothes washed in communal trough used for everything 'cos 'tis the only place to get water in the *patio*.

Spaniards cackle, make noise. Others sit staring, mind half on watching clothes in case they're nicked by fly-eyed desperadoes. I think of Jennifer, her quilts, warm room, pot plants, stereo. Her launderette visits on cold winter evenings and how it would fair if she really were—A Bear.....

Now music alters and falters. Judy my final emblem of you is going up in smoke. Blown out everywhere, the ring I have held close to me for 3 years now wends its way into the Moroccan mountain, with a little bit of me in the slipstream. If you came to visit me I might feel a little guilty—But I doubt it, knowing what I know and anyway you won't come and visit.

The Russian "stateless" person, talks to me about the Jewish race. Someone once told me that the Jews invented Christianity to sell to the world. 'Tis possible such alchemy I suppose, such power, such vision, such exploitation into the moment, of a particular Time/Space, in order to glimpse the in/finite in the in-finitesimal, and see what is and hence what will be and has been, in its entirety.

I don't know, just speculation in my own limitation, trying not to go too far out and blow it all. I guess to all intents and purpose I've gone through some sort of breakdown in social terms. I've thrown away every chance I had, crossing my path, my fate/line. My main/line—

Giving up autumn's warmth for winters wandering in desolation, miles from home, under summer sun-skies, with spring fading in the silver mists.....
- Ceuta—Los Rosales—June 18th 1979—
Evening time,
Darkness—Round the corner.
Fifty six pages. I'm proud of that. Even with editing, reconsidering and rewriting. Fifty six (seven now) pages is a lot of pages of sweat, toil, blood, life. The hardest things I have done in life have all been connected with writing.

It's like someone wrenching in your stomach, up to your heart, into your throat, up the back of your head and pulsating a grey mass in harmony with space/transmission; then regurgitating the message through the whole being whilst hand, part of which is pen, scribbles out a constant scream of signs/symbols that we define as

Language

Communication

A break,

From the dissertation

Very bad stomach ache this evening, could well be the food. I eat mainly dry bread. Erie night noises from Moroccans *brigada*. Screams, shouts, anger from next door. Wail of cats in far off alleyway then almost complete silence. Two flickering candles. Frenchmen playing cards their voices low like the light. Suddenly from somewhere much noise, banging, raised voices drifting through moonlight. Creaking doors.—An eerie note floats across the world.

Hope I get out soon

Before a new moon.

Hope that I make it

Through the night.

The Frenchman who was crying this morning told me about himself this afternoon. He is 38 years old, a salesman from Lyon, married, and with a ten year old daughter. The hashish in the chess set was put in his car (so he says), without his knowledge. He wrote, telling his wife, expecting some help. She replied telling him that she left him and wanted a divorce. She'd told his whole family and he'd lost his job.

What a loss for someone, whose family will never know what it's like to be stripped naked, Exposed,

And have only yourself

For comfort.

Where they switch the water on the tap drips. As it falls it bounces on the granite—A billion molecules, bursting apart and joining again.—One of the wonders of the world, water. A molecule or an ocean.

I talk with the Englishman, Clive. He has been here a week and is confident of a quick payment of his bail.
Last time I was in prison I met a Clive. He came to me to meet a spaceship in the sky.
Cold winter day, ice on roads, bright frosty star shine. His hand points out a faraway light—"It's getting nearer," he says.
One day it picked him up, took him, asphyxiated, to other lands—Elsewhere.
And a part of me aided his blast off
A part of me went with him,
A part of him was left behind
This Clive, though, is different. He has an agitated gait. Nervous gestures, good writer though he is, he has much "To Comprende".

Clothes drying in the breeze; slow gust of silent dust. Life written in shadow-land casting slow silhouettes across sunshine. Time for a shave.
I guess the Drug Rehabilitation Unit will assign my present situation, if they knew it, to loneliness. Not being able to sustain, or make new relationships and in the end I had to get away, from my own feelings. Block them out is the therapeutic expression. I wonder possible maybe 'tis so.
When you've pumped you arteries,
The blood-river inside,
With alien bodies,
They can't get out
They linger
Perpetually swimming the rivers.
Loneliness, Guilt—I am more welcome in this world than I am in the other; for here there is no loneliness for me, no guilt.

I live by my wits, drink the energies of contemplation
So I may face once more
The world of alien being.

I remember, you, Cassandra Cooper. We arrived at the Rehabilitation centre on the same day. We were peers. You small dark sensual. A queen of the northern soul circuit who sold her body for the feel of dicanol in an ankle vein. You drew two pretty flowers by your signature; indeed all your writing was gentile, stylish, pretty designs of lines.
Yet what a slut! How I remember after a year of therapy, your flashing knickers on my eyeballs as you crossed legs. Your whispered fantasies. Our Mutual masturbation after lights out. Grinding your crutch on my sticky fingers. A bud of sexuality. Insatiable desires. I remember you, Cassandra Cooper and the fear in your eyes.

Rudi has depression. He holds his withered arm. His face is grey with disillusion as he tries to find a reason to carry on. He must see the Consulate and doctor, about physical condition. I, too, am run down, tired, stomach ache, high pulsation in blood. Endless flow of "No Problem" from British. Fly buzzes round me.
Hope I get out soon,
Back on the road again,
Footloose and fancy free.

A new French Sputnik arrives. A 'croupier'. He looks like my dead friend Clive. Same coffee coloured skin. Tales of other lands from traveller's mouth. I lose my pen but fortunately a new one now flows 'cross page.
Drifting wind;
Silent sins,
Conceived

Rudi has aching arm. It feels like stones in the stomach, one kidney, he tells me. Wonder what its like pissing with one kidney?—Bad enough with two. Day passing slowing. Fly playing in shadow world. Waiting, waiting;

For the Sun.....

It was only fourteen years ago, according to the French 'Sputnik' that the Moroccans started making hash, they were, apparently taught by the "hippies." What a coup for whoever made such magic. Strange tales from this stranger who has had many voyages and survived. A meeting of wanderers; shadows on shadows, moments on moments, in moments—Canary Call—A picture of Einstein with fairy stars in his hair on the cover of TIME Magazine.

The Moroccans catch flies by not disturbing shadow. It is the only way to ensnare one.— A hippie, mountains, West turning East; teaching religious mountain men the magic of hashish, so they may spread it elsewhere. Loud snorting laughter from the French. English eating onions reading comics.

Read, read, read. See the letters on the page. Look care/fully. With full care.

Stare at these signs on these lines

For this is no faery-tale.

Albert Einstein's birthday fell on the 14th March 1879. $1+4+3+1+8+7+9 = 33$

Say no MORE. 'Nuff said.

Bit odd really. Strangely strange yet oddly normal.

As they say—A co/incidence.

Skin dry from blazing sun. Hottest I've known it since I got here. Head pounds, dry mouth, stomach tense with under nourishment and stabbing pains.

Ceuta sun.

Clapping hands,

Drift of voices,

Faraway places,

Spaces beyond.

Rudi says that today was the end of a dream for him. Reality slashing his sight, like steel through wrists. He looks old tired, grey, lined, passing through shadow in another land, unknown to this time.

What I mean is that moment when you're not there. People talking all around you and you don't hear a word, you're somewhere else completely and then you return, to what ever you were doing, listening to the T.V. or the conversation......

"Oh I must of been miles away," you say. Like Rudi, only his contact with that mythical "miles away" is more realistic than someone whose mind, just drifts for a second.
Rudi may drift for eternity
On the ocean of e/motion
Aware of his journey
Miles away in time and space.

Thinking of Wilfred Owen's "Strange Meeting", with a dead man. Rudi says that, "Life is with him as long as he feels the blood course, in his one good arm"
A biscuit here tastes so good, as does coffee. Nine swigs of steaming hot, sweet, black, syrupy coffee in one day to sustain oneself. Cigarettes I can't afford. Relying on the odd coup with a shirt to pay my debts
Sip debts,
Joint debts.

I always provide candles. A valuable asset like this manuscript.

I have a roll for breakfast. A slice of bread for lunch and an orange. Today my bread had maggots and had to be thrown away. The food here is awful. Tasteless yellow beans with a lot of excess water. Meat is horse or dog served cold. Hot water is an unknown. I've had one shave in seventeen days. Only really good thing here is the hashish.

Wondering if anyone will pay up for me. Then what? The mountains maybe or back to England in disgrace ?

This I say with a sulky sigh,
No more heroin for quite a while.
Make music, make songs, right wrongs
But no more heroin for a while
Or it may destroy me with a smile !

I guess, what I'm saying is that in recognising my "junkie mentality", I also recognise its shortcomings of how far out to actually go, without toppling completely over the edge. Places like Ceuta, or the Rehab save my life in a way.
Snoring noises filter through the windows
Last cigarette glows in semi light.
Whispered conversations
The French
Planning their futures
In shadow.

A brand new day. My job as assistant brigada cleaner pays no money, but gives me a daily bath. I feel fresh after long wash in soapy water. What a treat! Sky really deep blue, almost like a deep blue ocean. By midday the whole *patio* will be under the glare of this heat. We are in for what my Mother would call a scorcher.
For the second time today I am on my own as far as sight goes, although I can hear the sound of bamboo bristles across granite, as an orderly sweeps the remains of breakfast, into the primitive drainage system.
Hoping today to maybe get some news
From the other world.

Sitting in the cool shade near the centre, waiting for my second shave in 18 days. A Spanish legionnaire makes faces through the bars of his solitary cell. Sound of demolition, shatters concentration.

Hoping that soon I'll have paid
The price to Ceuta
So life may move elsewhere
And this story will be told.

Unfolding the map of dreams before me. Loosing the crap inside. Songs that come to mind. Lovers left behind. Leaking brain, resources drain. Weak from using too much energy and not sustaining the output/input balance.

The *Functionales* sit in the 'Centre;' talk furiously, with animated gestures. They are all prisoners of bureaucracy, ruled by the rules of the administration ...
Unaware of their confinement
Their position in the game.

I dream of the Mountain—The "Montagne."

Something mythical in Ketama. Maybe that is where I will go when I leave here. To see for myself its magic. Exchange spaces in Foreign Lands.

I have a vision of my Mother somewhat perplexed by my movements. Cutting flowers in the back garden. Wheezing a little, eyes watering perhaps a few drops are tears. She listens to the wind, the crocuses, the bloom of Surrey summer, with her son far away. A sigh for lost dreams. A little breeze. The house is her home. Here she will stay secluded, patient,
wise
Whilst her son travels on

Another voyage.

I think of my junkie friend Malcolm, dressed in jodhpurs, turning over a manure heap. Mucking out paying for his sins. Light-hearted, with humour, he perceives my plight. Slightly puzzled he doesn't give it much more than a moment's thought, before continuing with the next little Stow on the Wold Stable job.

My Father maybe moved inside on hearing of my situation. The final straw perhaps before total disillusion. Yet an awareness of hope. A glint in his eye, like a star in the sky, reflecting on the sea. My Father, thinking back over his own memories, flicking back the pages of his own history. His travels on the seas to the Antarctic, South America. The ocean, its depths below as the sky above, his own moments. Aware that I experience my own, in my own way, which is different to his own, but which he will always be a part of because he is my father.

It's as if, in spirit, I'm actually with them. In the sitting room, watching the solemn faces, influencing the final outcome.

Thinking 'bout the future, in deep blue dome of the hottest day I can remember, since I don't know when. Weary, drained, sipping citric water in cool shadows. Really slow pace here, never felt so laid back in many ways.
Wasted
A/Trophy

Here perhaps the most precious of jewels is water. The Spanish wash their feet in the puddles near the wastage. It looks an exhilarating experience, for most water is sucked up by sun's energy, returning elsewhere. Here a trickle is a stream. A pool an ocean. Evening brings a brisk, sunshining breeze, sitting
With my clogs on
Trousers rolled up past my knees,
Sweeney Todds T-shirt

Round my head,
Doubt if I'll have much more than this when I get out,
If I get out.
The conversation continues,
Here, in myself, and elsewhere.

Fading rays of day—Army's harmonica's harmony, crosses the trembling world. Sunset like the razor red sky. Prison blues on my mind and maybe I ain't worth a dime, to no one.

My Mother, thinks I am. My sister, will be unsure but quietly compassionate, as always. My Father, will be wishing he was back at work and will dispense drinks all round. My brother, Jeremy, will hopefully be on my side. Day sets on Dorking town.

Number 3 she wear a frown
Cross her sullen brow
Dark business inside
A ride on the roundabout
A spin on times turntable
To weave my web
My time.
But maybe I delude myself. No one debates my position.

These evenings peacefully glide into the jaws of moon/time.
Night's realm spaced across the horizon.
For Venus, the first star
Light the candle,
With humility
To its humble presence,

And watch it blaze
Into power like a bud from a seed,
To spread light.

Last moments to-day and my crystal candle holder is smashed in half, by poorly placed feet and head, in bed next to me. Been elsewhere, most of day. Manana, out of sheer desperation I continue work here. Voluntary work without pay. Maybe I'll get a letter tomorrow. Some news from another land.

Utterly depressed this morning. Feel totally rebellious, want nothing but to get out of here. No money, no dope, not funny no hope. Don't want really to even write, feel like throwing down my pen and saying—"Enough is Enough!"—Now I want just to do nothing. I want to lie on a beach in the sun. Gently roll into the sea and then sip Coca-Cola, in the cool shade.

But reality is this courtyard. The dirty smell of human wastage. Crammed spaces. Writing words, in sunlight and shadow, as a form of penance.

It will be very hot again today. You can tell here by firstly, looking South over the fortress walls at the Atlas mountains. In the morning their clarity, coupled with the amount of birds in the sky indicate the weather. Cheaper than a B.B.C. licence. Today; the mountain shone with clarity and carrion birds, scream in flocks - Above.

Day scorching. It is so hot I'm hardly capable of writing. Tiny little flies. Guess it must be over 100F. Even the shadows give only slight comfort. Light cover, from naked fire.

Had a bath this morning. Can't remember much about it. Athletes foot bad. A refreshing "Douche" in cold water. A comfort for its harsh clarity, a million tiny shots of water, splay the body. Manana. Manana. Manana.

Clive, the Englishman who broke my candle holder last night, has bought me a packet of cigarettes in compensation. Nice gesture, obviously feels bad about it. *C'est la Vie*. The crystal obviously meant to go the way it went. Hoping to hear today. Something from outside. Beyond the walls of Ceuta .

The two French brothers are poor. They read books incessantly and like myself, beg a few sips of coffee or coke to sustain themselves. I wonder how they feel together. What sort of relationship they have. Maybe they exchange a lot more than books. Obviously, they share goals like all good smugglers. I expect the older brother feels responsible for the younger one. I know I would, if it were myself and Jeremy here.

Flies everywhere. The baton waving legionnaire whirls his weapon in the air. Sound of water dripping, from a hole in the wall.
The heat has brought out flies in their thousands. I wonder if they give you diseases. They snap at ankles. Everyone is drowsy from the heat. Even getting up and walking round to relieve the monotony brings spots to the eyes.....The forces of fire.....

Still wondering on England. I guess today will be retrospective for those to whom I've written. Slowly fading anger, retrospection, nostalgia as life goes on. At least I'm not there and hence physically affecting the situation. I'm 2000 miles from home, my Mother muses, as she stoops to cradle a flower.
Anxieties playing on my mind. Outside the main perimeter of the prison they are building a new wall. The sound of invisible workers and machinery enter this poverty and poetry, to strain the mind.
The mail arrives. None for me. Perhaps Manana or not at all. I go up to the *brigada* for Siesta time.

Somewhere canaries call. Their song disturbs a motionless sea of silence. We feast on a sandwich of lettuce, garlic cloves and bread, washed down with squeezed lemon and water. Black tobacco stabs the back of the throat as the humming generator starts up, pulsating through the heat wave.

What can I say? That I didn't say yesterday—Can I say the same thing in a different way? Or am I writing only what has been written before in a different way ?—Rimbaud, Artaud, Blake, Yeats, Eliot, an infinite list of writers who in their own Time/ Space have perceived their own vision.
Their own writing on the wall.

Sweat gathering on forehead. Only the linoed floor offers some respite from the inferno.
The day for us prisoners dies, when the sun falls behind the Western dome of the old fort.
Relief appears at the final point of solar descent. The *patio* becomes bathed in shadow, allowing the sun drained body to drink in tranquillity. Another day goes its way.

Here in Los Rosales sunset whatever time of day it occurs, is the end of day and beginning of night relaxation. It comes with a delicacy, invisible to the naked human eye. Day's pounding red heat fades night wards, on a twelve bar blues played by the moon.
Not like London.
(Day/Night/Night/Day) = DAY or NIGHT.
Whichever way you wish to see a succession of time. In the city, night or day, there is the thud of mechanics which is no more than a misunderstood fascination here. In Ceuta air and water rule. In London, synthetics, by products, and consumerism make the most dramatic impact. Neon's, electricity, car noises, a constant scream of relentless synthesis—24 hours a day/night.......

Nearly time for the whistle to blow. The summons for sleep. I await with the French brothers, two Englishmen, and the Spaniards I call Tweedle dum and Tweedle dee. I note at a distance, the Spaniard who bought my 'Jean Machine' shirt. He parades his new attire proudly, thinking he got a good bargain. He sits on the bench attached to the wall, behind the archway. He doesn't look well suited to the shirt, nor it to him. He is too skinny and the arms of the shirt too long. The tail hangs around his thighs, in an ungainly fashion. The whistle blows and we march to the *brigada*.

Day sleep, night awakes,
To take over
The Watch.

Nineteen days now and I'm aching to get out, before I get brain damage from the climate. The sway of the way to nowhere. Feeling deserted in a desert. Maybe here will be a rest home. A living graveyard, some unsung hollow in the pit of being.

Or maybe I'll make to it the mountain
With the aid of my allies
Bailing me out
From Ceuta....

The Noises die away and the Harmonica plays. It is party time. Bruno switches on the light. We gather for mint tea and hashish. Taffy, the Welshman, has made a good deal and he shares his good fortune. He makes a good impression of a happy man. But inside he battles with feelings of despair about doing 7 years. He stares blankly into space. He wanders and wonders, barely comprehending this foreign land, his forehead lined. I've caught him at times, twitching.

Soft murmur of talk. I lie on my bed dreaming of Oxford. Cumnor Hill, The Rehab where I had my head shaved, and cut logs with a broken axe in a dirty boiler suit. Hands cut, from splintered bark. Shouted at, and shouting at. Paying penance.
Taffy wouldn't think so. He would like Cumnor Hill with its rolling hills. Its glades and woods, dappled gold in autumn glow.
The glum glow of electric's. The thought of coffee round the fireside. Warmth whilst winds wage war. Pull my hat over my eyes. Sleep will come.

In the *patio*, this early morning. Clive, the 'writer' and arrogant Englishman, who has only been here a week, tries winding me up.

"I don't know why you bother with that writing. Waste of time," he says. "Its a load of rubbish what you talk."

"As you don't hear anything, how can you comment," I reply.

"Why don't you shut up them."

Joseph the Russian separates us from a fight. I really feel like hitting him. Retire to a corner. Wounded.

This Englishman Clive, reminds me of Tom Masterton, whom I knew in Maidstone Gaol, some four years ago. He has the same twitching, swaggering gait, and red beard. Thin. A bit Gollumish. Slimy and insensitive. My mind goes back to 1972 driving down the Cromwell Road with Tom Masterton. He had one of the first briefcases ever of organic cocaine. We thought we were groovier than the Pop Stars who grovelled at our feet for our wares. We attracted the wrong sort of attention. C.13, drug intelligence unit. Tom Masterton was busted at Heathrow that autumn. He received 7 years for 8 ounces of cocaine. I met him in Maidstone gaol again while doing my own sentence for hashish. In Maidstone we forged a friendship. One day he gave me some hashish to look after. I was busted in the gaol losing four months remission and spending 38 days in solitary. It changed my life his sacrifice of my time for his own.

Geckoes have appeared outside the *brigada*, slithering across the masonry in the sun. The sun. Reminding me of this other gaol in another country.

How Tom Masterton had flayed his fists at me, when I accused him of 'grassing me'. Summer, in the English heat, as we walked around another perimeter, another *patio*. Two middle class Hippies, under the microscope of the criminal fraternity.

"So, what are you going to do. Smack me !" Tom sparred menacingly. And, I taking aim, firing my force at him and him tottering, unbelieving. His hands going up toward his blackening eye. Slamming him, and that part of myself that I loathed and saw in him. I punched on Tom Masterton's face, the whole part of the social structure I abhorred, and renounced it

On a cricket Pitch,

In another world,

Before this time—Began.

Feeling rebellious again. Wanting to get away. Slowly, oh so slowly runs the sun. I am lost, lonely and breaking under the pain of life. Deserted, hiding like a fly in shadow.

I wonder back again.

Tom Masterton's Mother moved to Ireland after his incarceration. She bought land in County Mayo, hoping to hide her shame. His father was dead and maybe Tom went there to live with his widowed Mother. Maybe he farms, quietly looking back, on how illusion became disillusion. Remembering faces, written on cornfields, or milk churns. Haunted by dreams.

Or maybe Tom Masterton got out of Maidstone and made his dreams come true. Cocaine smuggling, running borders with $20,000 in his pocket.

Poor Tom Masterton where are you now ?

Rio de Janeiro ?—Or underneath a cow !

Afternoon siesta. The French play *cartes*, argumentatively......

Actually am totally run down. Lowest ebb point of a tide. Suicidal almost. Fed up with the grubby little games of life, of having to play the loser or the fool. I suppose somehow, somewhere, some peoples get something from my existence. What a 'blow out ' I am—A whitewashed example of failure, sitting in the evening sun, scribbling,

when all I really want to do

Is cry and die.

In order to be free of pain.

I sneeze. The sniffles returning. An incessant semi cold seems to haunt me. No news from anyone either. Justifiably seem forgotten.

I should have stayed doing the degree at college but I didn't. I threw it all away and left. Exchanged one way for another way and this way appears madness. Nowhere to go even if I do get out; although somewhere, maybe, there is some place where I may find a little peace.

Somewhere in 25,000 miles there's a place where I may be accepted.

Keep writing; Write on you bastard ! Keep the pen flowing. Still alive so make use of every moment. Let it flow whilst it can. 'Tis only out of ugliness that anyone can perceive any beauty. This is the main reason, I guess, I 'm here not at college, experiencing middle of the road contentment and building up responsibilities. Maybe I would be happier that way. No doubt by now I'd have probably qualified for next year and be well on the way to some success in Academia. I might have a lover. Someone to cuddle up too. Tonight, instead of this flea ridden *brigada*, we'd wander down to the Pub in the sunshine, drink lager and eat crisps. On the surface I'd be doing very well.

Yet inside

Knowing that all I was really doing was

Cheating the Hangman.

Playing out time.

An ineffectual beacon on a road leading nowhere.

A social sèll out

Who knows what he's done and how self deceptive he be....

Flies on the *patio*

Geckoes on the wall

Listening to the laughter

Waiting for the call.

Dirt 'amongst the granite

No tarmac on the floor

Waiting in life's windows
Death's dream 'cross the door.
Faces fit the movie
Walk out on the scene
Play the part you're paid for
Find out what you be.
Director, script writer, producer, star or walk on part.
We all make up the whole
With our souls.

I wish linguistics wasn't such a problem although I guess I'm quite international now. I talk passable French and communication by signs other than words a big asset. Get on better with the foreigners than I do my own kind. Bit sad but reality.

You don't need to verbalise pain 'tis written in the maps upon your face, in the oceans of your eyes. One look from a stranger of empathy, says more than a million words in one's own tongue. A recognition of the world inside, which each and everyone of us deals with in our own way.

Sumi, asks to read this manuscript. He reads attentively throughout siesta time. When he has finished he says to me "You write not for one but for all. The whole of man... You understand ?" He looks at me pleading for comprehension of his analysis.

Today in the heat I have suffered with my aloneness, with desperation, with total negativity. Yet today, earned a jewel from this man who actually read the words on the pages, for what they are.

To you Black Brother,
I give thanks.
For your words have given me the courage
To carry on.....

All in all not a very nice day. But tonight seems more *Tranquillo*. No shouting or real outlandish noises in the *brigadas* . Only outside prison sounds. A loud television, muffled by different murmurs, distorted by distance. Echoes in the silence, these nights under foreign stars. Just for one second all is peaceful, and I turn my thought to the Cap I've acquired, which I wear on my head. The whisper of conversations. The distant oasis behind the sun. A chess game. Shallow, nasal snoring breath.
Myself
As a part of all being.

Ugh! Ugh! Another day and the pollen count is very high. Terrible sneezing and eyes watering from irritations. My new hat given to me by Rudi's friend, Norbert, defends my head against a cauldron of sun. Sting of fire on shoulders. Scent of sleep in morning air, drowsy with heat.

I guess the Christian fantasy of hell was similar to this. Incessant fire. A ball of endless burning.
Hell could be the Sahara
In all its glory.
Or Hell could be Ceuta
When I'm feeling poorly.

I seek solace in the shade of the arches, listening to the noises of mid morning with my nose dripping, from histamine.
My pen runs out. Finally. Thank you ink for supplying so many pages of this notebook. Ninety eight to be precise.
Siesta time and once more, I receive no letter. Manana perhaps I will hear. Doesn't seem to be that important really.

It seems more valuable to have written almost 100 pages of words that all interconnect. Have a relationship from beginning to Now... This ending;

A landmark

For one who has dreamed of this very moment in many, many schemes.

I have written 100 pages in order to prove to myself. There is no real reason. I have just followed various signs, ended up here, writing incessantly, hoping to maybe find something out through the words I write. As a reader, may find something out by reading what is written.

Its something to write about in the hot, Ceuta, siesta sun, with a royal blue sky and the sleepy atmosphere of another day in this tranquil world. Writing about 'rites', on the lines of time. Feeling fine in the mind.

Today as I write on my hundredth page of a manuscript for the first time in my life.

There is a rumour that some of the Spaniards, Moroccans and Legionnaires, have typhus. Have to be very careful with what to eat. At the moment my staple diet is water with squeezed lemon and mint, a small piece of bread and hashish. I wonder what I'll do when I get out, whenever that'll be. One of these fine Mananas.

Perhaps it will be autumn with seas angry and winds wild. Or maybe still shimmering in summer's energy. We shall see. What will be, will be, said with resignation against the background of another fading day. Wind play in triangle of remaining sunshine. Looks as if the drainage hole in the middle of the *patio* has got blocked. Not a good contemplation. Flies abounding. This Los Rosales is a difficult place penniless, 'cos 'tis impossible to contribute as much as one is given. I sell another shirt to elongate a few cups of coffee, for our group. We share eagerly the murky liquid, for its flush of energy.

Only when it is cool can I write now. Cool enough for my mind to run through the back pages of my memories. Replays. Video recordings in glorious five dimension, of past, present, or future moments. The invasion of sun's naked glare, makes presentation of such word/ mazes impossible, almost; for sun sucks up the energy, so that one is drained of any ability to think clearly. To seek beyond the spots, behind the eyes.

Have decided, to write on the other side of the page when I reach the end of this notebook. Unless, of course, fate has in store for me some surprise that may overcome the impending problems, relative to paper. I doubt it. Day, will move on to night. Night, back to day. Manana will begin again and the words will still mark the pages. I will still be here watching the time slowly sink away.

All the money in the world cannot buy back time. Money has little power, in a place where men wait out their lives in this dusty Spanish outpost. The only really valuable commodity is hashish, whose particular type of dream staves off the pain of being.

A new Frenchman appears with a guitar. A brand new toy in a world devoid of such triviality. He is no player but has a secret compartment in the neck where he has hashish. It is shared greedily. We all have a go at playing and I rate reasonably highly.

As I play, the chords take me back, to Beaufort Street London S.W.3. My friend, Giles, with his white Gibson guitar, long angular face, and aristocratic nose. His girlfriend, Camilla, small and petite with a well rounded face and determined eyes. Here I plonked my first two chords, as a rudimentary accompaniment to Giles's wailing notations. Beaufort Mansions 1971. What a space, none of us knowing what we were doing, just doing it and suffering the consequences. Endless nights with guitars, stereos, cocaine, razor blade, making the magic that changed our lives. Long ago now. Under special Chelsea lighting we dabbled with unknown crystals. Not caring from snort to snort. All for one. One for all.
Till we fell.
Destroyed by some unseen construction that our way threatened. The slow descent. The night I went to visit Chris Cans, who lived on the river by Battersea Bridge.

"Couldn't you see your friend on the boat. A bit of brown powder, to come down," Giles's persuasive voice.

How Chris Cans filled my nose with his brown powder. Then returning, walking up Cheyne Walk as my feet seemed cushioned by two inches of soft foam between feet and ground. Head washed warmed by a soft storm of swirling clarity. Gut and emotion quieted like the controlled glow of an internal peat fire. Taking back this first packet of heroin. A little one with Giles. A little one with Camilla.

The first time and the last time; in that, from that moment onward, we had tasted forbidden fruit. We were doomed to be its slave. We became bitter angry, hateful. Guitar plays.

I remember you Camilla, eyes trained to the sewing machine's movement. Pretty cloth all around you. Still stuttering from the childhood rape that left you speechless for nine months. Your fingers made the most beautiful shirts I've ever had with those little needles and pins I never understood.

That first line of cocaine I gave you.

"Tha..Tha...Tha..That's far too much Ro...Ro..Rocking..." I winked, sardonically smiling as I passed you the twenty pound note. You were never the same again.

All those mornings spent in pain
All those nights high on cocaine
The disillusion searching in vain
For keys to turn your life insane.
Reflect like diamonds in your eyes
In this dying world someplace to hide.

Last Line Chapter ⑤.

For you Camilla, in this book, a poem of beauty. All you've ever wanted from me.

Still the guitar plays.

End of day,

Out of tune

Echoes down the corridor. Footfalls on the ground,
Silently.
The reflection, mirrors another reflection, only.
Soon it will be soon.
Sleep around the corner
Senses lighten, towards unconsciousness.

Today we awoke to a heavily overcast sky. Like England. The hot weather broken by a rain threatening sky.

"It will rain till the full moon tomorrow night," predicts Joseph. His Russian correctness gives an esoteric inflection to all he says. A double innuendo, of perplexing thoughts, over a simple statement. Wind gusts against body. An unusual occurrence this grey filled sky.

Today will be hard for me. No money no funny. No dope no hope. First drops of rain reach paper....Cold....Cold....Cold....

Taffy the Welshman tells me about the riot they had last year. It took them two days to get it under control. Afterwards, at night, just after the *brigada* lock up the *Functionales* came. They would randomly pick ten people from each *brigada* and they would be led to the *patio*. Here their hands were tied above their heads and attached to posts. Each one would be whipped till they screamed for mercy. Taffy said the screaming was worse than the whipping and it continued for eighteen days. He bears the scars on his back. Not the nicest of stories to digest first thing in the morning.

Tears around the corner. Feel like crying 'cos no cigarettes, food, money nor hashish. How can one write under such conditions ? Blocked head, aching bones and hoping that I may, eventually, feel some sort of reward rather than punishment. One can hardly consider Ceuta in murky grey with absolutely nothing, a den of creative power, when half ones mind is obsessed with consuming something.

I am called to the Centre where a *Functionale* tells me I go for my Tribunal tomorrow. I am happier at finding the pen I lost. Hopefully things may now start to happen and some moves can be made to get me out of here. Rudi has found a smoke and shares with me the joint. As I puff, a ray of sunlight splits the cloud bank. The newly arrived Frenchman with the guitar offers me pineapple juice. I take a sip. A burst of unused taste buds as morning wends its way towards lunch. Sitting here wondering what's going on in the other world. Drainage system stinking. The French chat idly in the gloom.

Bruno the Italian reminds me of Peter Carnegie. They have the same aloofness and large nose. I remember you Peter Carnegie, for cocaine in the mornings and the Acid trip you once took with Tom Masterton, in which he thought you were God. Rising ten foot above the ground, brilliantly illuminated by your own aura. I remember you, a head of your time, a wizard, who now after the electric shock treatment, remain singularly confused by all you've ever done and even Tom Masterton would have difficulty, seeing you as God.

Feelings of remorse. Thinking about what might be when I've left here. No money, no clothes. Taffy, suggests I go and work on a farm he knows in Ketama, making hashish. Not a bad idea but I suppose I must return to England and face the music.

The last page of paper that I brought with me. No money to buy more, nor ability to get a decent type. Ha ! I am nothing. No more than a pimp, a thief. My only distinction from any other junkie is that I have this strange relationship with words, or think I have.
All I wanted ever to be is myself, yet to have the freedom to be myself is not permitted. Thus I have learnt compromises, travelled the roads I have travelled to end and begin, here in this moment of time/space reaching for the last line of paper on which to write a word.

Begrudgingly start with writing on other side of paper. Lowers the value of the original manuscript! Everything not quite so neat and tidy. Still I remember in Horseferry Road dungeons, where I languished for three days, after Clive Jones had died on the kitchen table, writing on toilet paper, words written by a soul

caught in two worlds, so to speak.
Trying to work out
Which way to go.

Seen in this context writing on both sides of the page isn't such a problem.
Tomorrow I go to the Tribunal.

Back in the *patio* after the Tribunal.

What the Fuck anyway ?

Magistrate speaks : "Cinquante Mille Pesetas. " (50,000 pesetas.). This I assume to be Bail money.

I make a gesture at my tatty clothing...."Vingta cinquo mille",(25,000), I bargain as advised by my fellow inmates.

"Cinquante," says the Magistrate sternly.

"Vingta Cinquo. Por Favor." I once more plead.

"Cinquante. You 'ave family."

Cinquante Pesetas, it is.

Recollection interrupted by noises from the Spanish *brigada*.

What do people hold in their heads anyway ? Asking me to pay the Spanish Government to let me go. Like the Mafia, or people's fantasy of what the Mafia is like. Get yourself a country, grab dope smoking foreigners, and then demand a ransom from their family and friends.

Tears. No letters. What now ? They say not to worry. There is a postal strike in England. Don't know whether to believe it. *C'est la vie.*

"I have a dream," says Rudi. "In my dream I sell my car. I go to the woods. Sit under a tree and overdose. What is there for a one armed junkie man ? Nothing but death." His voice trails off.

Rudi dreams of a release from pain. He hopes that there is something beyond hopelessness. Maybe there is nothing, but even nothing is better than living in a world where people appear crazed with making bull shit, and doomed to destruction by their own insensitivity to each other. The inability to see themselves, as part of a whole.

Each and everyone is told, that there is a top and bottom to that whole, and that the passport to the highest rung is money and power. The bottom is failure, total disaster. Deviancy. To be at the top means you are more important, perhaps, to the whole, than if you're at the bottom?

Nonsense.

No Top. No Bottom.

A Top. A Bottom.

If it is that there is a distinction between the two.

And, surely, the sum total of humans being,

If it could be represented

Geometrically,

Would be a circle.

Or do we believe that humanity is a ladder,

Flat

Like people thought the world was, centuries ago ?

This morning on the way to court. Rush past people, Moroccans, Spaniards, Tourists, Ceuta summer time. A town in crisis. The Police were jovial as were the people who stared blankly at my handcuffed hands. A prisoner of a regime. Caught in no mans land. Paying the price for playing the fool.
For having no desire to be at the top or the bottom.
Indeed not even being able to recognise the position of either,
On a circle.
Anyway I don't think people are really interested in the shape of humanity. They are, each and everyone, too concerned with their own lives, to recognise they are no more than a molecule of the human whole.

Headache, feel weak. If I was on junk now I'd feel as if I was really desperate for a fix; i.e. at the worst point of a come down. Sick with sun, bars and blue skies stretching to eternity, instead of being sick for the feel of morphine in my brain.

Legs weak, head pounding, mouth dry with thirst and lack of nourishment. Day slowly, slowly turning its circle.
A circle ?
At what point on the human circle are you now ? Maybe you're at the top, or think you are.
A Director, Sales Executive, Lecturer at Polytechnic. A Doctor, Dentist or Politician.
Maybe you're at the Bottom, or think you are. Coal miner. N.U.P.E. worker, Shit House cleaner, criminal, drug addict.
I wonder if you did a survey which of these various groups would admit to having what George the Frenchman calls "A Cosmic Glimpse of Eternity?"
Probably only the drug addicts and some of those would probably side with the others, and would consider your question less valid than your sanity.
Nevertheless, someone might have "A Cosmic Glimpse of Eternity" in the depths of deprivation which might appear to them, more valuable than £10,000 per annum,

company car, wife, children, one of whom may have their own "Cosmic Glimpse of Eternity."
An individual should be given the freedom to value himself.
"If there be a judge let that judge be you. You are only as valuable as the value you value yourself at;
Not what anyone else tells you is valuable.
What you, yourself, cherish about yourself
'Tis to the Human race, as priceless
As the rarest diamond.
Valueless or invaluable advice ? I wonder. Pen scrapes across paper. No letter today. The Spanish Government values me at 50,000 pesetas. A price for Freedom.
What will be will be.

I wonder if I'm allergic to hashish pollen. I take some of the golden powder and press it in my hand. I roll and knead it till it turns black, malleable and smokeable. It seems to get up my nose.

Many of the people here play some very childish games. Understandable I guess, boredom resulting in regression to Prep School type behaviour. The latest of these cruel sports is 'bait the Black Man" i.e. Take the piss out of Sumi because he's convinced that death is near. I don't get involved but the other English join in the general bullying.

I have nothing now. No cigarettes even and I'm getting used to the hollow empty feeling in the gut from a lack of food. Indeed have almost given up smoking cigarettes, occasionally cadge the odd drag here and there but nothing which could increase the chances of cancer. The little shop has opened and most of the others have gone for goodies. Still no doubt I will have my chance, when and if I get a letter with a £1.00 note in it. For Tuck!!!

I remember it was the same at my boarding schools. Never enough money, always begging half pennies, beyond any reasonable level of credit. Hoping for more than enough, rather than enough, 'cos enough, (however much it be), never seemed quite enough. If you see what I mean. You aim to get a house. You get a house and then find you want a better house. Even if you have three of everything, you will want to go forth and get a fourth.

Something most people consider a natural thing is the competitive spirit. Free thinking, liberal Democracies throughout the Planet, base their society on such logic. That people will always want "more than enough." After all, they are brought up to believe that they are entitled to it. Those endless technological machines to which we've become enslaved. The T.V. and the washing machine. All forms of labour saving devices for us to consume. They (We), not really 'We'. I don't subscribe to the I.R.S. of Britain or America. I pay nothing towards maintaining the system. Hence the system treats me as an outcast. 'Tis so. Prisons, rehabilitation centres, anywhere but the streets. But not 'We', 'They', is the correct pronoun. They build their world on competition; that the physical self, its maintenance and potential, is the ultimate in life.
Whatever the cost or loss to the Human whole (Hole);
The gyre of Cosmic Being.
Enough ! Enough ! Enough for now ! Of the philosophical moment.

Canaries call. The Spaniard who bought my Jean Machine shirt has received "Libertat" or "Freedom" to us English. He stuck out his chest proudly this stringy rag and boned Catalan. His eyes betrayed his vulnerability and sensitivity. He wore the shirt proudly, his bag across his shoulder. No more with which to face the world.

Had a beautiful wash this afternoon. I took three buckets of water and stripped naked, standing over the toilet. One bucket to dampen the body and soap it. Then one over the top of the head, followed by a further massage of the body and hair, with soapy shampoo. Then one more bucket of icy cold energy, to shock one into the recognition of what it is, to be gloriously clean.

End of siesta. Time for the evening sun before dinner. People settle into reading in the shade or basking on the stone benches. My hair dries in the soft breeze. Two more French smugglers arrive today. Half the *brigada* is now that nationality. They occupy quite a large portion of the space of the *patio* here. Writing on, birds chirping, waiting still for some word, some salvation so that I may have something, however little. One day, I guess, I'll be free.

Manana, Manana, cry the flying objects whilst I sit here patiently in the sun. Thinking about coffee, about England now with summer time bursting across the buds of the last spring blooms and the hot city steaming with people.

I remember last summer. I drove trucks everywhere in England. Full of tropical fish. Hot clammy heat, sweating as a labourer or worker, from 7 in the morning till maybe eight at night and a third of what I earned went to the I.R.S. of England. Still whatever you do you pay, one way or the other and governments as we all know, must be paid for.

Not that last summer was all bad.
Evening sun on Cumnor Hill. Tranquil, mellow glow. Faraway gleam of light over lakeside. Staring at the sun's slow descent through French windows. Sipping coffee in a soft armchair. Dreaming. Strangely content, sometimes, when a rush of love let itself burst in my heart, and I wanted to let everyone know how much they meant to me.
Warmth
Close the door
Shut out the Emotion
Here in Ceuta sunshine
Cold
Rules.

Again the drainage was exceedingly smelly today, although have changed my clothes and feel personally, quite clean. Slow winding down of day. Waiting for the whistle to blow us up to the *brigada*. Sky orange over the mountain, burning silver sun splayed over horizon. A foreign prison with a foreign sky to stare at. A window to the world.

Oxford with your dreaming spires, I think of you, of the nice placid existence I might have made for myself in your city. Playing at being a cured Junkie, when every morning I would wake up and wonder why I'd exchanged my junkieness, for humdrum middle of the road life. Riding on buses, pretending to be a potential academic. Trying to accept ideas I'd rejected long before. Making a mockery of myself for the benefit of others. Surrendering. Better to be locked up than play such a game.

Evening dry, golden, driving out for a drink in the countryside. Watching trout jump by a swirling river. Hoping I was on the right track when I wasn't really.

That me being rehabilitated was a farce.

For I was never habilitated in the first place.

Yet I learnt something of myself and other people in my time there.

When the wind blows hard on winter nights and tapping twigs tickle glass, then I will stare into fires, and recreate all the faces of that time, with joy.

A fire of human warmth in the optimism of regeneration. Hoping for the future that the rehabilitation would work. Toiling the land, chopping the wood, washing up, running a kitchen, being shouted at and shouting at. Loving and hating, despairing and trusting. I remember you Cumnor Hill for all the help you gave me.

Taffy paces up and down, his brow furrowed.

Night heat.

Sway of moonbeam from afar.

Looking out at a star.

Thinking about all that went before this time so I may try to find a way out of my present predicament. After all, I am only the sum total of all my previous experiences. Nitter natter, in my mind. Pitter patter, down the corridors of time. All these thought are an unwinding for me. Disconnected ramblings through what occurs in my head, when pen is in hand. In many ways, it makes no sense. Except we all live in our own, unique, worlds of 'disconnected ramblings', flying cross our own planets, in every moment we be, in whichever way, that moment represents itself.

Be it Ceuta Gaol.

An afternoon playing golf

Or watching television.

Wherever you are

You experience the moment of now

Simultaneously with everyone else who is...

Or be

Alive or dead on this, (for me), hot sweaty "Los Rosales" night, back being tickled by blanket, head buzzing with soft murmurs. Cap pulled down past eyes. Ready for sleep.

Few light drops of rain. An incessant pounding of a pneumatic drill from the outside. Rain getting heavier. Time to dash inside before paper, gets drenched.

Another day, another doughnut.

One of the Legionnaires has a salamander in a jar. He chases Sumi with it. One bite, they say, and all your hair falls out! Sumi is justifiably petrified. The Legionnaire apparently has given up his chase. Obviously he has had enough sport watching poor Sumi's eyes, turn white with fear. Suddenly, he darts towards Sumi who screams and runs into a corner. The Legionnaire genuinely loses interest. He returns to paddling his feet in the overflow from the drainage system. The salamander safely ensconced in his pocket. Awaiting the next game in which he is used.

Yesterday, this same legionnaire produced from his pocket, a very motley flightless, baby bird. He let it hop around the *patio* from group to group. The bird acquired a meagre dinner of flies and pre soaked bread. Then one man picked it up. The Legionnaire put a piece of hashish between his lips, the bird pecked, like it was kissing its master. Everyone laughed. The bird was put down and stumbled about the courtyard. Stoned.

With my last ten pesetas I buy a coffee that after two minutes, disappears with the aid of thirsty mouths. But to buy ones own coffee, rather than be a pair of greedy hands makes it taste just a little bit better.

"Marchesi. Consulado." Comes the call. I barely recognise my own name. I look round. The Quasimodo shaped blue band from the Moroccan quarter beckons me with his one eye. I follow to the centre and am shown into a clean room. Here I wait. Hands tremble as the pen skims across the paper. Could this be the first step to Freedom ? Or to further lengthy incarceration ? Or nothing ? We shall see in a matter of merely moments. My hands tremble with expectation.

The consul enters. He looks clean and young. He carries a brief case and is accompanied by an officer. The one who oversaw my beating.

"Have you a cigarette?" I ask.

"Keep the packet," he says handing me twenty.

I light it quickly drawing in the smoke as he continues:

"Your bail's been paid. I have some money for you. I'll meet you outside the gates as soon as you collect your gear." His tone is matter of fact. We shake hands and I return to the *patio*. In a rush I gather my belongings from the *brigada*. There is no time for even some quick goodbyes. I don't dwell, fearful they will change their minds.

Suddenly I am in the town of Ceuta. Coffee with the Consul who gives me 10,000 pesetas. Unknown faces, places with no names. I bump into the man with my Jean machine shirt. He sells me a large piece of hashish pollen which I conceal beneath my cap. I make my way to the ticket office and board the ferry for Algecerias. The funnel hoots. We cast off. Africa disappears. Free.

Thank you Mother

Thank you Father

For without your aid the thudding beat of this propeller, would be the beat of the unseen pneumatic drills on an unseen tarmac, mixed with the thundering chatter of legionnaires, passing time, till they too received Liberty. Waves wash the boats bow. Children play in sunshine their laughter a liberation, free. The *patio* exchanged for the world. Wind whipped seas splash mementoes of Rudi and Sumi, of Tweedledum and Tweedledee. Their faces floating in the foam, written in this gap between Europe and Africa.

Life for me carries on till journey's end. Writing words, travelling on. A stranger in a strange land, be it prison or this boat pulsating through the waves, with spray of sea kissing my skin and tears of praise, for all those who saved me.
Here I have learnt the first lesson in years.
That above all one must be free.

Farewell Mountain I have watched sunset for a moon's cycle, round your con caved rockiness. Judged weather by your stories.
Farewell Angel of Death, Legionnaires, Moroccans, and Spaniards. Farewell, Bruno, Massimo, Taffy, Clive, Jean Marc, Norbert, Rudi, Joseph, and Sumi. Farewell wicked patio. Games of linguistic mis comprehension. Reading words in eyes. Mists of wind whipped seas. Farewell to you all. I take myself.
Elsewhere.

ALGECIRAS. Nothing 'cept sea and sand, as far as the eye can see. Peace. Tranquillity. Mechanics cushioned by evening's prelude. Whish wash of water on rocks. A Fisherman, cigarette and ball of thread in mouth, weaves patterns for his net. A Fisherman, a small boat. The window of the sea.

Remembering my Mother's tale of the little rowing boat, which acquired an outboard motor. It enabled the rowing boat to get revenge on a speed boat, that brutally splashed it when speeding past, calling the little rowing boat names.
Mellow evening sun,
Softly, softly dies a day.

A woman in red walks by. Beautiful. Like the wisps of water rippling in winds. Where to now I wonder ? Home to face the music.

Sorry.
Sorry's sorry
Forgiving forgives
Excuses excuse
But if you abuse, you will be abused !
Don't forget;
Forgetting
Forgets.

Manana the Consulate. Manana Mother. Telephone. The way back to England. Tomorrow I go back to another world. Bureaucracy, passports, consulates, Mother, Father, reality. Sad to leave this story, with all its glory. Night to day. Day to night.
Right to Wrong
Wrong to Right.
I give you this story;
A glimpse into another world...

June 28th 1979.

Part 2

MISSION

Nearly twenty years later, *March 11th 1999* I found myself travelling on a Virgin Express train to Heathrow, with plenty of time to be apprehensive about my itinerary.

The flight to San Francisco left London at eleven in the morning and arrived at 1.30 in the afternoon Californian time. A journey of 10 hours in real time but in man made time, only two and a half.

I was flying to California to meet X. a young artist, now 27 years old. During 1996 and 1997 we had worked closely together for a well respected sculptor, T., who subsequently invested in X.'s career. At my crumpled age of 48 my influence on X. was of a paternalistic nature, though we mutually developed under T.'s guidance. We drifted apart when X. went to study visual arts in Germany. In September, 1998, I heard rumors about X. having a drug problem, but I dismissed them until that is a fortnight ago, when I received a call from T. who angrily informed me that X. was:

"Running around San Francisco, hocking equipment I bought for his art to put heroin in his veins!"

My heart had dropped at this news, far worse than I imagined and I felt obliged, morally, to assist. Within a week of co ordinating this rescue mission I was booked on a flight to California.

In 1979 I dealt personally with the same drug addiction X. had now acquired, when I left London and went to live in Los Angeles. It seemed ironic, that twenty years later my return to California once more involved this unresolved opiate, which has plagued generations.

I had no address for X. but he knew of my imminent arrival. Telephone exchanges with him indicated an apparent keenness to disentangle himself and a desperation, as to how to address his habitual agenda of heroin. We agreed to make contact through a mutual friend, who lived on Haight Street. This name, conjured up mythological images from my long forgotten Sixties youth. 'Haight', to me was 'Ashberry', and it meant flower power.

Neither film, nintendo, nor music soothed the drone of that 747 flight. Each abjectly failed to distract my many internal anxieties. Even whiskey only helped a restless momentary doze, before surreal dreams interrupted by the smallest disturbance invaded my rest, jolting me back to 550 miles an hour. With an agonisingly slow velocity our plane flew over the North Pole, then south down the huge expanse of western Canada before finally we crossed into the U.S.A.

I was suitably exhausted for landing and immigration and dazed started my mission.
I had arrived at another dimension with a blank piece of paper, which I intended to fill.
The following morning I began:

Saturday March 12th

Awoke with a start at 6.00.a.m. in flash hotel near Daley city
San Francisco.
I attribute my very bad headache to jet lag.
A quick calculation reveals
I have slept barely six hours in the past forty eight,
Or is it fifty seven ?

I hired a car.
Took a trip to Haight street
The British Bar
Drinking with Londoners,
Who volubly recant
The woes of drug addiction,
As they sniff persistently,
Downing whiskies
Frozen and glazed.
When X. arrived,

We left without any farewells
He took me to 24th and Mission.

Wandered in a daze after this encounter,
Losing my car in the process.
Its scary
A strange city after a long journey
Looking for an automobile
Right in front of the eyes,
As unrecognisable as the air.
Somehow I stumbled on it
In a moment of recognition
And swiftly drove out of town to this hotel,
(Another vastly expensive experience),
Brought fully before my hollowed eyes,
This morning,
In the blackness of another world.

Still tired, though ate a good breakfast
Wolfing it down
Like there was no tomorrow and wishing I had taken more.
Yes!
I forgot all about this ritual American style.
The morning virtual feast
An open display of U.S.A. colour.

Still jet lagged;
My mind at one velocity,
My body at another and yesterday was a big day regarding X.

I think back;

The journey up to Haight
Meeting expatriates in ex pat bars
Wheeling and dealing down their own line
Reassuring me X will be joining us soon,
My ex pat companions disappear
To powder their noses.
X appears,
He seems okay
Though furtive, pasty, wan,
Relieved our mutual acquaintances
Are otherwise engaged.
Tired I follow him out,
Though when I went to the liquor store for ciggies,
He wouldn't accompany me.
He boasted of his prowess at stealing alcohol
With a specialisation in champagne and rare whiskies.

Again that shadow
Of internal anarchy
Passing his profile,
In the yellowy,
Hepatitis stained lights of America.

It reminded me,
So much of me
From my equivalent time,
When I stole my way through a heroin habit,
Twenty five years ago
And now clean,
With my own credit cards,
I wrestle with the same problem.

Jet lagged.
A head or behind by 9 hours,
Or in my case,
Is it twenty five years?

We drank whiskies
In a darkly lit bar
Near Van Ness
Conversation tense
Taut and tight
Both of us wishing to be elsewhere.
Relieved I sensed X.
Becoming edgy for a 'hit.

"Nothing can be done at a weekend X."
I said, making my excuses.

We arranged to meet Monday
At an ice cream parlour on
Haight street.

X. slid into the night
Smiling at the down and outs
Before slipping out of sight.
I went looking for my car and couldn't find it,
Panicked
Got disorientated,
Finally stumbled on it
Haphazardly, and very relieved left the city in a haze
Driving south till I nearly dropped

And without care
Found this Inn.
A huge Marriott style expensive place
Hosting a conference on Alternative Therapies.

It was like seeing my old self again
A rippled, wind blown, reflection
In a usually still lake.
The waters of life
Their transmutation
By the bottle and blood,
Those subtle traces
That weave us in.

Molecules of an ocean,
Humming birds.
In the motor
Our organs,
In isolation
A simple possibility.

Oh friend!
Down on Mission and 24th
Fight your demons
With the souls
Of your forefathers,
And the might
Of your Mother's blood.
On which
One is born
Not just to Earth

But heaven,
And to suffer
Ignobly
Down this spirit of nations.

Yes.
X. grasped by the velvet claw,
Seduced by Medusa,
Not quite but nearly
Swallowed
Whole......

i'm alive today
Standing
Ground
And
This precipice
Down which
i stare
Shakes me
With its knowledge
Of my own
Mind.

And
If i'd
Been accompanied
By the digital dot
Would my fingers
Arms, eyes and mind,
Have made

The same patterns
Performed on these pages ?

Time to make my way to Santa Cruz.

From the Hotel I rang an old friend M. who had emigrated to Santa Cruz, a town about 100 miles south of San Francisco. He left London for a new life and love eight years ago and coincidentally, had returned to London for the first time a month ago, when he had contacted me and introduced me to his wife, Z., and their family.

M. and I had been close for a quarter of a century. From the early 70's to the 80's we had shared squats and fallen for the same girls. Our own heroin addictions had crossed swords, as well as much philosophic exploration and some creativity. It was these dabblings which had drawn us together as much as their frictions were responsible for throwing us apart. On learning of my whereabouts in Daley City, M., immediately invited me to stay and I accepted his kind offer. Over the weekend I explained the nature of my situation.

Z., M.'s wife, dispensed advice as deftly as she mothered their 18 month offspring.

"It sounds like a tough cookie and I wish you luck but I wouldn't hold out too much hope. In San Francisco, Mission Street is down and out," she passed the baby onto his father's shoulder.

"Isn't Jack the cleverest child you've seen ? Someone really special," observed M. as he cuddled his only son and heir.

Z., who had borne two other boys now 8 and 12 from her first marriage, displayed the legendary efficiency of the Californian female as she organised her house.

"How do you know your friend wants to stop ?" She inquired studying her tax returns and musing: "He needs serious advice. We should give Mike a call. He'd know what to do. Where this guy could go to get off heroin. We live in a different culture here...He should be eating herbal remedies and drinking Detox tea. Does he have medical insurance?"

"He's got nothing other than a habit," I stated blandly.
"Good idea," said M., ignoring my comment while reacting enthusiastically to Z.'s. advice. He passed young Jack to his mother and strode, purposefully, over to the phone.

Within fifteen minutes we were sold on the idea that X.'s best course would be a stay in 'The Camp', a local rehabilitation centre where a course of detoxification lasted from 5 to 30 days dependent on finance. It was not cheap but being a cultural nomad, I agreed to their sound advice on the matter and determined to present this alternative to X. as a *fait accompli.*

On Monday morning, surrounded by the comforts of California, armed with varying expense sheets for the cure and convinced that a course of detoxification was necessary before X. could even think about getting on a plane, I left Santa Cruz to make my way to the city.

I was mesmerised by the huge expanses of sea and land, still jet lagged and juggling finances like a man in the options market. Once in the city I met X. He agreed to the plan but wanted twenty four hours to get ready. It seemed a reasonable request so I returned to Santa Cruz, still calculating the costs of my proposals, writing late into the night:

16.3.99. Santa Cruz. Aptos. 1 a.m.

Reflecting on today,
(yesterday now), and its repercussions.

The long drive from Santa Cruz to San Francisco.

The rock fall on the P.C.H.

The long wait for the road to be cleared.

Meeting the two Irish lads on Haight Street

And they expressing doubts about my chances,

As suddenly X. appeared.

His tall, thin, ungainly frame wrapped in a long black overcoat.

His pallor showing different hues of pastiness,

Talking the genre of his kind

A breed led by different types of whites,

Browns

The kulture of lemon juice, citric,

Whiskey bottle tops

Needles and kits.

Mexican

Chinese white

Mythological powders

That open Pandora's box,

Mesmerizing the user into believing

Without that little 'plasti pak' syringe,

They are nothing.

Only its pursuit and legend

Is worth a damn,

Or a dime,

In such a god forsaken landscape.

After all

Why not pollute oneself internally

Be a slave to the poppy and not democracy ?

If only it were possible, this Kubla Khan of existence,

This Xanadu.
The pinned eyed societal anarchic
Has created a prison of amoral proportion.

It got boring
Listening
Being sucked, into the sleaze.

And in every
Constellation
There is a
Mirage
As in every
Star
There is
A world.

Oh Pleiades
Sparkle
On
In your belt
Of Orion

For the red planet
Is here.
An inanimate
Of the
Institution.

17.3.99.

Early next morning I set off again. This time my agenda was unerringly straightforward. To pick up X. and drive him to 'The Camp'. It seemed too easy and so it was to prove, but before reaching San Francisco my confidence was high enough to pull in by the ocean and write:

Here by the sea.
The Pacific booming
All the way from China
To California
With its white pounding surf
In the full sight of Spring.

There is so much space for people here
A huge grand canyon of sight
From San Francisco to Santa Cruz
On the hardly used P.C.H.

Route One
Stopped on a deserted sandy beach
With the sound of breakers
All the way from Asia
To this
Here
Now.

Its a busy piece of advice
Buzzing in my collar,
And the whole phantasmagoria
Of X.,

Down on Mission and 24th street
And I,
To take him to
Detoxify,
Be dried out,
To prove his will.
Where is his will power?
To day I must find out
For nothing
Can go on
Forever.

If strength and will
Combine,
An unnecessary weight may be pried
From X.'s back.

In this optimistic vein I travelled up to the city and spotted X. fidgeting with his dirty shoelaces, in a small square opposite McDonald's on Mission street. He signalled an acknowledgement as I pulled into a parking spot on 24th. He sauntered over casually with an air of arrogance. His wraith like, sallowed features, emphasised prominent cheek bones bulging in the facial structure. His eyes were dark and pinned. Long dishevelled hair, hung over a forehead that poured sweat. He wore torn, paint splattered, combat trousers and a lewd, ripped, T Shirt. He opened the car door, nonchalantly throwing two bags onto the back before his body slipped into the passenger seat.

"That's my life. Lets go." He stated defiantly.

"You look terrible man." I remarked turning up my nose. He stank of stale perspiration. "Are you really ready to get outta here ?"

"Yea." He reached for the safety belt before suddenly he let go and it slid back to its holster.

" Oh Christ. No. I forgot. Look R. Remember that Liquor store ? The one you went too that first night ? The thing is the owner, he was really good to me and I still owe him $50.00. I owe for food. In fact I'm not going anywhere till I've paid him."

"C'mon X." I said, doubtfully.

"Seriously Man. Please. Give me the money. I'll pay him off. You can watch me. I need to get some clean clothes too. It'll take 20 minutes max. I promise you. He helped me when I was a starving man." Tears welled in his eyes. He began opening the door.

 I weakened. "Half an hour max. Don't let me down " I said, handing over the dollars. He was gone in a flash.

'You fool', said a thought in my head. 'Why let him go when you had him?'

I waited for three hours. I searched the area. He had disappeared into the downtown labyrinth. As I left driving south, the pale bleak sky added to my emptiness. Each way I looked failure appeared and my only comfort seemed to be in abandoning the whole project.

I quote from my journal:

Now I'm not one for giving up on anyone,
But three hours on Mission & 24th
Awaiting a junkie to appear,
Is more than enough
For this locally spun boy.
No!
Being left for dead,

By an old friend,
On Haight and Masonic
Or downtown by,
(S)mac(k)donalds,
Has alienated any of my offering.

Its once and once only and there is no immediate retraction.
I know from my own experience,
That the kind of kindness
I have on offer
Ain't for the taking
So I can't offer it anymore.

One can offer forever,
But lack of receptivity
Makes it devaluing to offer oneself
And have it knocked down.

I remember,
After waiting two hours longer
Than the twenty minutes
X. had told me it would take to pack his belongings,
Resolving to abandon all if X. didn't appear in 15 minutes.
He didn't,
And I felt taller somehow,
For my refusal to remain.
Why waste energy on one who doesn't want it ?
Coming down from my own illusion,
For I feel some delusion,
In my hope to have done something for X.
And now

My impotence and naiveté
Seem as bright as the beacon
On the P.C.H.
A lighthouse
The commiserate object
Flashing
As we all wish
So hard
To flash,
Be a Beacon
For some one
Some time.
A beacon
Of
Light.

And how much of this detachment
Is formulated,
By an association of my own identity
Of some quarter of a century ago ?
When I must have been as devious as X.
Or the devil
In my own pursuit of this no nonsense cause
With all its affectation?
And after all
Who were those
In my life
Who sat at telephones and awaited a realistic call.

Oh Monterey Bay
With your horseshoe mouth

And lips on Big Sur.
Oh Ocean
With your broken bones of flint
Smashed by the almighty
Pac
I
Fic.

Oh idolise this water
Before God
And let the filtrated
Demons
Be washed
So clean

By your
Golden Gate
That the solid might
Of my own
Entombment

May overshadow
Your slither
Of time
On this Marin County
Of soul.

Oh Jesus
With your candle lit
Procession
Be akin

To my own intentions

And let this
Candle flame
By the wick
Of my own indignity.

This night
On a half moon bay
Before the
Pacific and San Andreas
Fault
Make their line

In the middle
Of your
Main street
Artery.

I am
No more
Than
A machine
That
Reconstitutes
Air.

You arsehole X.
For abusing
A

Rite
Given
In
Purity.

I shall act out my own enigma
By the parking lot of another serendipity
Over by Main Street
Left of the '711'
Closer to the highway
In the looseness of my own gown
With the spilling surf
Calling, calling, calling,
Like my own Mother's ghost-:
"Life's hard enough why make it any harder ?"

Oh St. Patrick
Today I tried
To climb
Your mountain

But the Croagh
Of your shingles
Prevented me
From surpassing
Your summit.

I look back
On forest
Not forward
To Clew Bay

And
America.

Oh
St Patrick
Give me the strength
To have faith
In
Your
Beliefs.

"I hate to say it but it's what I expected. I knew he wouldn't come with you and leave his downtown junkie pals." said Z., knowledgeably. It was late the same evening and my humility was complete as I explained the day's events to my hosts in Santa Cruz. "You should never trust a junkie. I admire your sentiment and what you're trying to do, but really it's a job for professionals." She added with conviction and I felt foolish.

"Well, R., you must of expected it in your heart of hearts. After all it's probably what you or I would have done 25 years ago." Broke in M. laughing off my obvious discomfort. "You can stay here for the week," he continued cuddling Z. "It'll give me the opportunity, to take my wife for a meal one night while you baby-sit."

Then he added, more darkly: "It's been quite disturbing this reminder of a time one would like to forget. Who would have thought, when we were in that state that we would be where we are today? In fact, I don't know how I dealt with it. A night cap?" He concluded, pouring me a stiff whiskey and sensing my disillusion.

Before sleeping I wrote on:

And what of my own junkie spirit.
Where has it gone

Into Native Indian cigarettes
And home grown marijuana?

What of the slithering, sliding
Artful dodger,
The lodger
Who defies all
And makes a mockery
Of any form of composition?
What of the fall
From grace
The realisation
Of one's own
Nothingness.
What of it ?
This small, parsimonious,
Piece
Of time
In which I occupy
SPACE?

You let me
Down
On Mission street.

You let us
All down
And made
Your Goddess
In the
White Poppy.

She was
Pleased by
Your conversion
To her health.

You let your father
Down,
He of
Emphysemic
Pain.

He was let down
By your nobility
To another
Family.

My children
Were let down
By my
Innocence.

Go jump
Off the
Golden Gate
Bridge
Heathen.

The mind larking
Summer
Is over.
Look how

A leaf
May turn
Before
You
Begin
A
Book.

I paused. Looked out at a carpet of stars. The quiet of suburban Santa Cruz engulfed me. I felt like a fisherman who had a bite on his bait but lost the catch through a slight misuse of the wrists, more a misjudgement than any lack of skill. There was a need to make another cast, more deftly, with a newer brighter fly in order to hook this elusive salmon.

I was touched by a wave of sympathy towards X. Ashamed, at my weakness in being put off fulfilling my task by such an obvious ploy. I blamed myself for allowing him to get away. The hugeness of the continent engulfed my tired being but I summoned up one more poetic observation for my notebook.
In Half Moon Bay
There are more shops
On therapy
Than food

And even
Banks have
That organic
Touch.

I note the checks
From the swollen river
Cascade

Over Silicon valley.

Oh computer chip
Yea digital dots
And thou infinite
Proportion
Propose to me
A highway
An inter net

Where I may
Catch
Fish
Faster
Than
A Masked man
Can deal
Smack

To an old friend
Down
On Mission
And
In need
Of being
Out.

18.3.99.

In the morning I informed M. of my intention to return to San Francisco and make one final effort to contact X. again.

"I thought you might change your mind after a night's sleep," he replied surprisingly sympathetic. There was a resignation in his voice.

Z., as he knew, thought differently. I was wasting time she thought and should forget him. The atmosphere cooled in this difference of opinion. I realised my continuing presence was not overtly harmonious to their relationship. The nature of my mission was, increasingly, a cause of contention. I was a reminder to M. of a time he wished to escape. We drank coffee politely and despite their reservations they wished me well before I set off.

Once more I stopped by the Pacific and took up my pen.

A final effort at
What to offer, or not,
Before I abandon this ship
And turn in regard
To my own children,
Far off in another land
Out of contact
At the mercy
Of their own Mother,
And I, asking
My own Mother,
To bestow
Her mercy
Upon them.

The ocean storms
Massive walls of white surf
Varying shades, overcast the morning.

I don't like San Francisco,
But Santa Cruz and Half Moon Bay
Are the way of the future
With their new age approach,
For those not on
Social security checks.

I make this my last effort
To help X.
Before redirecting my energies
Back to my own kind,
Who not only need me,
But feed me too.

The waves of the Pacific,
In the eye
Of my own
Storm.

I parked on Mission street, got out and walked toward the building where X. said he often hung out. It was a tenement block above a liquor store with no visible entry point. I tried an abused entry phone and it didn't work which was a relief. I was paranoid that once inside I was the perfect victim for being ripped off.

All liquor stores in America have their own brethren. Like fleas on a dog the 'brethren' wheel cart loads of aluminium cans to their 'doggie' proprietor who pays them a measly amount, enough for a shot of whatever their addiction, before they go off searching for further disused cans. Other more ambitious, sly, 'brethren' hang about doing doggy deals to get whatever they can, however they can to feed their habits.

On failing to gain entry I telephoned our mutual friend on Haight street. He told me X. was due to call and I told him to inform X. of my whereabouts when he made contact. I then wandered up a block or two where the pushers plied their trade. X. was not to be seen and I didn't hang out. As I returned to the car I saw, from a distance, the figure of X., in his long black overcoat and sneakers leaning on the car. When I arrived he stood straighter, as if expecting a verbal tirade. His brown eyes, full of a charmed sorrow, meekly met mine.

"Lets get the fuck out of here X. I'm not talking till I see the sea." We drove off in silence.

At Pacifica, some miles South of San Francisco, we stopped for coffee. I ranted, he raved, but eventually we reached a compromise. The Detox plan was to be abandoned on X.'s insistence. In return, X. was to surrender himself to my charge with all his pawned digital equipment, before taking the journey back to London. As I had baggage in Santa Cruz and it was too late to get X.'s equipment, I reluctantly returned X. to Mission. We agreed to meet early the next day.

I had driven over 350 miles before I reached Santa Cruz at midnight and without a note in my journal fell into a deep sleep.

Early next morning I said my final farewells to M. and Z., before making my way North for the last time. I promised to return before leaving for England but I knew I wouldn't. Whatever the outcome of that day I resolved to put Santa Cruz behind me with a great deal of gratitude. I had made it clear to X. that I could easily return to England without him and that fiscally this would be my most prudent policy. If I was again subjected to a disappearing act, I would disappear myself to Marin County and make no more contact with him.

In trepidation at demons of my own making

Still half contemplating my own kids
I sip
A double latte at Half Moon Bay
In the rain,
Half way to San Francisco.

Having arrived in the city, I parked on Mission street and waited for X. After an hour I decided to enter the sleazy building and find the apartment, which he called a shooting gallery. This time, I waited by the gate for it to be opened by another tenant. I wandered a labyrinth of dark corridors, before I luckily located the correct apartment door.

A young wasted acne-infested woman, with traces of a faded attractiveness answered my knocking and volunteered to guide me through a search of street corners. I could tell she too, was waiting and wanting X. but for opposite reasons to my own. She had a lightness of gait that suggested, at one time her lithe body could have developed into that of a successful ballerina. Difficulties and heroin had robbed her of any ambition or self regard.

Our search was fruitless and I turned down her offer for me to wait in the apartment, until he returned. I sat in the car for another hour before pacing the block in agitation. A junkie approached me:

"Say, you the English guy looking for X. ? He's a bad case. Tell you what he left real early this morning. Give me $20.00, I'll tell you where he is."

"Is it far ?"

"Ten minutes."

I gambled the money.

"334 Bartlett, just round the corner."

Bartlett's street numbers stopped at 370 and began again at 324. I had been conned. Taken for a sucker. In my mind it was the final straw. Marin County here I come, I thought, as I went back to the car ready to drive away. A dirty T-shirt and a digital tape were draped on the windscreen. As if sensing he'd pushed me too far X. had left these pathetic items as an indication he was about. I looked around and saw him walking towards the car.

We set off on a belated tour of Pawnbrokers, un hocking digitized equipment, filling the car's back seat with the latest hardware and software that Silicon Valley can offer. After this, by X.'s recent standards, gargantuan task, we went back to Mission street. As evening approached we finally set off for Half Moon Bay with everything intact and found a small hotel room. Only then did I feel safer.

My poetic journal, in time with the moment of that time, tells its own story of these moments:

Mission between 25th and 26th sitting like a plonker waiting for X.
I have visited his seedy little room with its junkie occupants,
Smelt the carpet on the stairway.
What a mess !
One step forward and two steps backward.
And the smell in the air of rain,
As my options diminish
With each second of the clock
The arrangement with hell,
That could be avoided with one turn
Of the car key
And the final haul up to Haight,
Or to wait by the stall

Patiently
For a junkie
Who might never come.

I walk between 24th and 26th.
One of the junkies from the 'shooting gallery'
Sends me on a wild goose chase looking for X.,
At a fictitious address on Bartlett.
This information cost me $20.00.
I return to my car and X. has left a video tape
And a dirty T. Shirt on the windscreen.
I once more knock on the apartment door.
X. opens it slightly, sweat pouring from his ashen face:
"I'll just be a minute man."
We gather together his hocked equipment and head South .

In the Half Moon Bay Hotel room which has no T.V.,
X. sweats in the bed the other side of a round table.
Its a nice town.
I'm not completely without sympathy for its
No smoking, New Age policy.
And tomorrow X.
Will be waking on his come down
From the poison.
It is a poison
This added extra to the blood,
Not just a plasti-pak
But a steel contact,
With the cut umbilical.
You will pay for this quarter

In the deck of your own cards,
But I'm not looking at capping
Any cosmic expense,
Not by the expedient of my own motivation.
A pity prevails,
For my own past life
And those of a future generation
Caught in your balls,
and not your bull shit.
Here, on a Half Moon Bay,
With the full moon
At least three weeks away
From sight.

Interesting to see how breath can be affective.
I draw in deep,
X. laughs
In his sleep,
Draws breath in.
Am I being breathed
Or am I breathing ?

20.3.99.

In the morning X. fidgeted through breakfast. We had collected most of X.'s valuables but there was more to do. I cajoled X. into arranging a transfer on his flight ticket by confronting him about his behaviour. He pathetically made his way to the phone. Yesterday, we had paid a liquor store in Haight street for the return of X.'s transferable ticket and passport. When X., returned from the phone having managed to re-book his flight for the following afternoon, I felt a warmth toward Tony the owner of that liquor store, who had shaken my hand and said to X.:

"You get back to England and get into treatment man. Before it's too late." As he'd spoken, he'd handed X., the transferable ticket.

Pleased by this flight confirmation we returned to San Francisco in order to buy a large case to store the computer. Having bought it, we discovered it didn't fit in the Dodge. This provoked a heated argument on the sidewalk outside Black Market Music. As we struggled to get the box in the car I lost my patience, insisting the case was useless and that X. should get my money back. X. insisted his hardware needed protection.

"Oh yea ?" I danced. "Just like when you hocked it and used it as collateral for smack! Really thought it needed protecting then huh ? Who the fuck do you think you are ? A Rock star?" X broke down in remorseful tears as I berated him for his complete failure to address this problem.

It wasn't till we calmed down we realised if we took the lid off the case, it would fit in the car.

Once more we drove to Mission so X. could stock up on 'Mexican wraps' to tide him over till he reached London. As he went about his business I continued the journal.

X. distracted, knows what he's done to himself
Shot himself in the foot
With all his equipment and his habit.
How many years will it take him
Psychically
To overcome this problem?

I shall be glad to see the back of Mission
And its wooden houses,
Shacks even,
Designed for an Earthquake
Rather than any form of aesthetic beauty.

X. has left something
In his junkie home.
He has jumped the wall
To climb the fire escape,
And enter the semi derelict building.
I am seated by a tray
Containing a damp dirty copy of
"Meetings with Remarkable Men".
A coincidence,
That reminds me I have not enjoyed this sojourn.

It's a struggle
And I wonder if X.
Understands the amount of patience I need
In order to just sit around
As he performs his junkie behaviour.
Like a marionette
The needle pulls its strings
On the puppeteer
And how the junkie dances to the pipers call.

I try to recollect myself in this state, but find it beyond my imagination,
That I'm the same person,
Who stole and abused from those closest to me,

So I too,

Could dance the dance,

Of the Poppy seed.

Jerk and wobble to its motion,

Then collapse in a stupor of remorse, at my own imprisonment,

Before the music of my 'plasti-pak' began its devilish whirl,

And like it or not,

It was take your partner

For the next fix.

The seedy junkie world,

A semi shadow

Where the body is only vaguely seen

The sombre shades of darkness

Protect one from the sight of others.

I grow weak on my own passed visitation.

The story close but far away

And my own distinctions

Mistakes and muggings

Right here

On Mission and 26th street

With the sun peaking

Thru' a cloud.

Some hours later after supper and time on the coastline,

Looking up at stars over the Pacific.

Noting how inconsequential one is,

In relation to such a vast phantasmagoria

We know as the Heavens.

X & I exchanging
Childhood memories
Of there being someone
On another star,
Living a parallel
Though opposite
Existence,
Which co incided
And was interdependent,
On our own.

New towels, new hotel.
Last day for X. in San Francisco.

21.3.99.

Cold morning in Half Moon Bay
Damp from the sea rising up toward the sun.
Fog Horn blows
Warning ships of an approaching doom.
On the highway, cars speed
North and south,
Down this most ragged of roots.
Expectant.
It is still in the wind.
The only movement being those of machines.
Here; Now
On this ball
Of
Miasmic

Power,
May the form
Be balanced
In
Thought,
Will
&
Action.
The very source
Of life
Holding one thru' a cycle.

We left at mid day for the airport after X. had spent the morning, wondering whether the sharpness of his hypodermic needle would see him through his journey. He hinted about having the time, to go to the city for a new one before we checked in. I insisted there was only one journey left for him in California, that was to the airport. I wasn't giving him another opportunity to get away.

When we arrived I left X. in a long queue and went to the bank. When I returned they were weighing the flight case. The expense on the extra weight of this luggage nearly led us to blows again. In the end we kept our cools and I handed over my Master Card, hoping it would still work. It did. The case departed and X. was handed a boarding card. We walked to the security check and said our farewells. I watched as he went through the metal detector and into no mans land. After he disappeared my eyes became mesmerised by the flight information screen. A green light flashed boarding for half an hour before it changed to a permanent 'departed'. Even then, I waited a further 15 minutes before being convinced he was gone. I left the airport and returned to Half Moon Bay with a sense of achievement.

I booked into a small inn overlooking the creek.

It grows dark outside

And clouds cover the top of the Black Rock Mountain.

I am totally exhausted, physically, mentally and emotionally,

Especially the latter.

Should I have known

My Mother's ghost

Would rise from the Pacific and dictate all proceedings ?

Should I be down on my knees to X.

For being a junkie ?

To his Mother whose experience,

So reminded me of my Mother's

And how this encounter,

Has as much to do with my relationship,

With my own mother

And that our sufferings,

Helped another Mother and son,

Come to terms

More gently

With what we had too.

And this gave the whole terror

Of our existence a meaning,

Some different substance,

Which may be

Has enabled both of us,

To be freer

In our respective worlds.

For if ever

I needed proof of

Life beyond death,

It was verified, when X.
called his mother in Italy,
And my own mother,
Her ghost rising from the Pacific
Gently brushed my cheek
With a kiss,
From eternity.
I look forward to her next VISIT.

Back to business and financial calculations. I have retained nearly all my receipts and I
have calculated an approximate cost, (vast like the rest of this country), of my journey.
It's thousands of dollars and I don't care to state how many.
X. must have been on the plane for nearly six and a half hours now.
I watched him through the security checks into the duty free area.
I watched the information until the plane had departed before leaving the airport.
I'm sure he might be looking to the inside of a toilet right now and hoping against hope
he'll be all right.
Still, I'm sure the next 3 - 4 hours will pass no more uncomfortably for him than any
other passenger on that B.A. flight. I wish him all the best and hope he makes it through
to London.

Another night in Half Moon Bay for me.
The cheaper end of town
Not the flash Inn that we stayed in last night
So X. could luxuriate in a bath
Get himself clean
For the first time in months.
No.
This is much more 'twee',
Homespun
Quilted breakfast, a small T.V.,

No ashtrays of course.

Now X. has gone
I start to wonder 'bout my own children
How they are as they trip their own light fandango.
How quickly the years of childhood go,
One anticipates each stage of growing up.
The first smile
Crawling, teething, walking, speaking, learning
And suddenly
One looks at pony rides
And children's playgrounds,
Realizing that
One's own children
Are no longer interested
In affairs of the playground,
But the affairs
Of the heart,
And I wish them all the best in these affairs.
Though they remain for me children,
The possessors
Of my memories
Of those earliest years,
Those never remembered
For oneself,
But which return for the first time,
In the sight of ones own children.
May they too witness,
The sand and surf
Along this noble coastline of California,
With the pride and dignity

Their lives have already earned.

I bow,
In reverence,
The dance continues.
Spin a long
The alley ways
Of indiscreet
Identities.

We have
A notion
It sees
The Ocean ality
Of our competence.
Let hope
Forever
Be present
In your chosen
Professions,
And may there be
Some gratification
In your
Endeavors.

The moon
On its initial quarter,
As I lay my head
In its Bay .

God bless you

Spirit
That
Guides
Me.

22.3.99.

In the La Di Da Cafe. X. has arrived back in England with all his equipment, so there is already some sense of achievement, especially in comparison to where I found my self last Wednesday.

I shall stay here now until the aeroplane tomorrow;

Maybe visit the Ocean one more time.

In this vast distance
Between Pacific
And far Atlantic.
In all the thousands
Of miles,
The millions of homes
And worlds,
Each the centre
Of their own universes.
Over these vast distances
To travel,
May be
Never
Returning,
To this tremendous
Coastline

On which my heart
Breaks,
Like the white horse manes of surf
On the rocky cliffs,
Formulated
Out of this
Collusion of land & water.
The fire in the belly
Of
A
New civilization,
This Californian
Peninsular,
Made from
Those May Flowers,
Sewn,
So long ago.

Thus 'amongst this culture
On the threshold
Of an new era
I bow to the spirit
Of my forefathers,
Who brought me
Through their struggle,
To here; Now,
This God given
Moment,
Of
Time.

The Golden Gate
Has opened.
It rains
In
San Francisco.

How amazing! The phantasmagorias of this country and all its inhabitants
Who live this new Kulture
Imbibed with teenage innocence.
I am no mean man making music in a middle eight
Nor am I letting a Nation off the hook.
It rains and Americans look out fearfully for the highway moving, precipitated by the
youthful exuberance of a newly formed land mass
Growling on its fault line.

This communion
Life gave me
Is a rare privilege
For which
I thank
All
I've ever
Known.

Back at the 'Twee' Hotel.
Room 27 as opposed to 28.
A fine mist like rain smothers the distant hills in a cloud bank
That rolls all the way down to Highway One and into the sea.
As a thirsty man drains
The last drops of his drink,

So after such a veritable feast of vision,
I eat my final fill before departure
Not wanting to miss a moment.
An enrichment seems a fair description.
The night and morning
At the Half Moon Lodge
Stars sparkling
That sense of Spirit
Being the embodiment of the power
Moving me here.
A debt has been paid to the Gods
A conscience has been cleansed
On both sides of the fence
A meeting has been made by remarkable men
Over this skilful drama of the stars
Playing like Pleiades
As they sparkle through the night time.

23.3.99.

"I'd pay that sir," advised the car checker when I mentioned the Parking ticket I had received on Haight Street. She calculated the costs on my Visa Card that she skilfully inserted into her hand held computer.

"It's been a good car," I remarked somewhat wistfully.

"I'm glad you enjoyed your holiday sir. Been up Lake Tahoe I guess? Have a nice day."

I smiled and left without replying to make my way to the terminal. Once there I checked in and went quickly through the security check.

The plane left on time and I once again followed the slow velocity of the 550 m.p.h. 747 on the T.V. screen map so kindly supplied by the airline. By the time we had made some progress over Washington state and were headed west over Canada the monotone engine had mesmerised me into an uneasy sleep.

Simultaneously in London,
Some nine hours later
Which of course
Is exactly the same time
X. threw every good intention out the window.

Like Dracula,
X. was sucking blood with his modern, plastic, hypodermic.
He eased the needle like tissue, through the skin
Into the blood river of life
It ploughed
Sucking like Dracula
Sucks the dreaming neck.
To feel the fix of teeth on his point of being.
X. sucked and the blood shot
Into the oily white brown solution.

"Drink sir ?" Asked the hostess.

I started out of my slumber replying in the affirmative. There was still a long way to go and I downed the whiskey in two gulps hoping it would lessen the discomfort of my economy seat. It didn't, but I closed my eyes and returned to my surrealistic pillow.

From royal blue red,
From the womb of X.'s veins

To the works
The alchemy of life
Tinged a little lighter.

X. for a moment stared.
He stared at the foreigner
To his being,
The little kinection
Between needle and body
With the plunger ready to shoot,
As tributary meets river,
River meets sea
Sea meets ocean
Heroin/cocaine
Met X.'s mainline.

This was not on the flight schedule. None of the digitized programmes of the Virgin 747 showed this interactive movie. I was a disturbed human being, falling in and out of dimensions faster than the speed of sound. My planetary location faltered as I sauntered between levels.

That very night smiling a skeletal smile
Baring a busted dream
X. pushed the plunger
And sent the solution flashing up the stoppers neck.

The foreigner invaded
A splash of milk white demon energy
In the pulsation of an artery.
The invader enveloped the whole.
X.'s heart quickened

His stomach folded
Face frozen
His mind reeling
Hands drooping
The fix over.

Like Dracula
X. flew night skies and moonbeams,
Sheltered from the storm of being.

Momentarily
He felt like a modern day demi god
Dealing in life and death.

He had planted the die
In his own game now.
The bullet
In his Russian roulette.

That night
On the darker side of Notting Hill
Far from the benches
Of Mission and 26th street.
The combination of too many fictions caught out X.
His head fell forward on his chest.
The needle still impaled in the crock of his arm.

Breath came slowly
Vomit coagulated
In lungs, throat and nose.

Solid matter dripped
From his orifices
As X.
Despite all willing
To be breathed
Succumbed to another realm
And no longer
Drew breath.

Time ran out like an hour glass. The sands of life shifted at 35,000 feet above ground. 20 years ago and now, merged into one linear, vertical time, rather than a straightforward horizontal. The notion of re enactment and repetition blurred, continuing distortions, which flickered like an old 16 m.m film sublimating my sensation. The Arctic circle and Iceland had disappeared in the slipstream.

"Are you all right sir?" The hostess awoke me with a start.

"You look pale. Would you like another drink ?"

"I'm fine thank you. A bad dream." I tried to shake off a nagging empty feeling. There was an acrid taste in my mouth.

"We'll be at Heathrow in 20 minutes," she said. The progress of the 747, a tiny dot on the T.V. screen revealed my closeness to home. I fastened my seat belt for the impending descent and for the final time wrote in my notebook:
This pen has reached its limit in the ink world
It ceases to flow
Is drying up
And as an empty shell will be added to these artefacts
From this journey
Into San Francisco.

I write like I'm writing
But did
I ever
Write
Before ?

Postscript

Unlike my dream on the Virgin Aeroplane, X. did not overdose and die but after the inevitable relapse or two, cured himself of all drug taking. He has resurrected his life and artistic career. He fell in love with a philosophy graduate. This May she bore him a son. X. has been clean for over a year.

EDITORIAL NOTE

Readers will inevitably recall the Beat Generation of the 1950's or the Bohemians of the 1800's—but this is no imitation of some past literary movement and its struggles many generations ago—this is today. The writing is strong, alive, and honest. The problems of addiction are unchanged. This book is not just a satisfying prose/poetry account of Mr. Marchesi's personal odyssey—it is an unintended clinical, historical, literary milestone— it is a purely modern story that unconsciously parallels brilliant drug addicted writers of past centuries, with the conclusion that their demons were real, that their anguish genuine, that their eerie road is today still dark and poorly charted.

John Cullen, Clocktower Books

ABOUT THE AUTHOR

Robin Marchesi was born March 1951. He was educated at London and Oxford universities. He travelled widely as a child and young adult. In 1990 his first book was published, A.B.C. Quest, by Cosmic Books. In 1996 he published Kyoto Garden, a book of poems, by March Hare Press. He is currently working on a book entitled: 'The Poet of the Building Site'. about the Sculptor Barry Flanagan.